0 031140 024816

# ROMAN M
## MYSTERY

# ROMAN MURDER MYSTERY

## MYSTERY

*The True Story of Pompilia*

DEREK PARKER

SUTTON PUBLISHING

*For*
*Kenneth and Arthur*
*at Toorak*

First published in 2001 by
Sutton Publishing Limited · Phoenix Mill
Thrupp · Stroud · Gloucestershire · GL5 2BU

British Library Cataloguing in Publication Data
A catalogue record for this book is available from the British Library

ISBN 0-7509-2582-5

Typeset in 13/16pt Perpetua.
Typesetting and origination by
Sutton Publishing Limited.
Printed and bound in Great Britain by
J.H. Haynes & Co. Ltd, Sparkford.

# Contents

Romana Homicidiorum – *nay*
*Better translate – A Roman murder case;*
*Position of the entire criminal cause*
*Of Guido Franceschini, nobleman,*
*With certain Four the cutthroats in his pay,*
*Tried, all five, and found guilty and put to death*
*By heading or hanging as befitted ranks,*
*At Rome on February Twenty-two,*
*Since our salvation Sixteen Ninety Eight:*
*Wherein is disputed if, and when,*
*Husbands may kill adulterous wives, yet 'scape*
*The customary forfeit.*

Robert Browning, *The Ring and the Book*

# List of Illustrations

# Dramatis Personae

Acciajoli, Cavalieri, confessor of the Confraternia della Misericordia

Agnese, a wet-nurse

Agostinelli, Blagio, an assassin

Albergotti, Bartholomeo, a gentleman of Arezzo

Angelica, a servant of the Franceschini family

**Arcangeli, Giacinto**, Procurator Pauperum, chief defender of Count Guido

Baldeschi, Alessandro, an assassin

Barbarito, Abate di Liberato, doctor of theology

Barberij, Giovan Battista, godfather to Pompilia

Batista, Angelica, servant to the Franceschini

Biondi, Angela, a midwife

Biondi, Pietro, husband to the above

Boba, Giovanna, a tailor's wife, neighbour to the Franceschini and Pompilia's wet-nurse

**Bottini, Giovanni Battista**, Advocate of the Fisc, chief prosecutor of Guido Franceschini

**Caponsacchi, Giuseppe Maria**, b. 1673, of Arezzo, accused of being Pompilia's lover

Caporossi, Barbara, godmother to Pompilia

Capozzi, Marquesa Panthasilea, a Roman aristocrat

Cecilia, servant to the Marchesa Capozzi

Celestino Angelo, Fra, Pompilia's confessor

Ciccaprovi, Signor, stage-manager of Roman executions

**Comparini, Francesca Camilla Vittoria Angela Pompilia**, b. 1680; m. 1693, Count Guido Franceschini

**Comparini, Pietro**, b. 1629, father of Pompilia

**Comparini, Violante**, b. 1632, mother of Pompilia

Constantin, Fra Nicolò, a confessor

Contenti, Maria Margherita, a prostitute and neighbour of the Franceschini

**Conti, Canon Giovanni Battista**, brother of Count Aldobrandini, Guido Franceschini's sister's husband

Conti, Porzia, sister to Count Guido

Corgi, Luc, a surgeon

d'Andillo, Fra Giuseppe, Principal of the Greek College at Rome

de'Rossi, Francesco Giovanni ('Venerino'), a driver

Domenico, servant to the Comparini

Fiori, Caterina, Pompilia's natural aunt

Franceschini, Fra Antonio Maria, brother of Guido

**Franceschini, Beatrice**, b. 1631, mother of Guido Franceschini

Franceschini, Gaetano, infant son of Pompilia

Franceschini, Canon Girolamo, b. 1654, Canon of the cathedral at Arezzo, Guido Franceschini's brother

**Franceschini, Count Guido**, b. 1658, an impoverished nobleman of Arezzo

**Franceschini, Abate Paolo**, b. 1650, brother of Count Guido

Gambassini, Domenico, an assassin

Gambi, Francisco, Procurator Fisci, assistant prosecutor of Guido Franceschini

Gideon, Dionysia, a witness at Pompilia's death-bed

Gregorio, Nicolò, discovered Pompilia's body

Guillichini, Gregorio, a young nobleman of Arezzo, distantly related to the Franceschini

Guitens, Giovanni, a surgeon

Innocent XI, Pope from 1676 to 1689

Lamparelli, Antonio, Procurator Charitatis, the attorney for the defence acting for Pompilia's estate

Lauria, Cardinal, a distinguished Roman churchman

Maddalena, the name of two of Pompilia's wet-nurses

## Dramatis Personae

Maggi, Abate, Canon of the Lateran Basilica

Marascelli, Abate, confessor of the Confraternia della
  Misericordia

Marchetti, Giovanni Matteo, Bishop of Arezzo

Margherita, a schoolmistress

Marzi-Medici, Vincenzo, Governor of Arezzo

Mattei, Abate Honorato, confessor of the Confraternia della
  Misericordia

Mini, Fra Bartolomeo, a curate of San Lorenzo in Lucina, Rome

Molines, Josephus, Auditor of the Rota

Mucha, Battista, assistant to Giovanni Guitens

Nerli, Cardinal, sometime employer of Count Guido

Olivieri, Agnese Santa, a friend of Angela Biondi, and wet-nurse
  to Pompilia

Panciatici, Abate, confessor of the Confraternia della Misericordia

Paperozzi, Corona, Pompilia's natural mother

Paperozzi, Cristina, Pompilia's sister

Pasquini, Francesco, an assassin

Patrizi, Captain Andrea, of the Roman police

Petronilla, servant to the Comparini, wife to Domenico, wet-
  nurse to Pompilia

Romani, Tomasso, uncle to Count Guido

Romano, Fra, a priest at Arezzo

Rospigliosi, Giambatista, Duke of Zagarolo

Scarduelli, Antonia, a Roman wig-maker

Scarduelli, Ursula, daughter of Antonia

Serbuceri, Giovanni Maria, Count Guido's lawyer

**Spreti, Desiderio**, the Advocatus Pauperum, co-defender of
  Guido Franceschini

Thomatus, Joannes Domenicus, Auditor Curiae

Tighetti, Domenico, trustee of Pompilia's estate

Vannini, Canon of St Peter's, Rome

**Venturini, Marco Antonio**, Deputy Governor of Rome

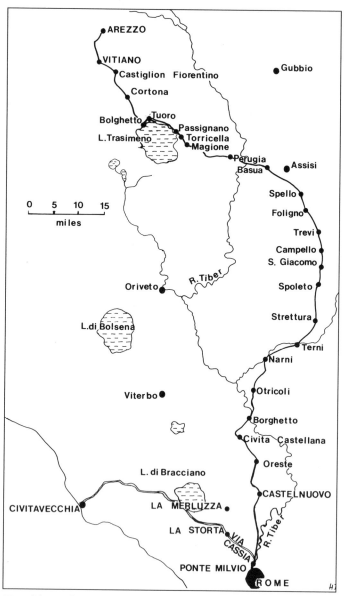

Map of the area between Arezzo and Rome as it was in the eighteenth century, prepared by Helen Livingston.

# Prologue

*Let this old woe step on the stage again!*
*Act itself o'er anew for men to judge . . .*

The place was Rome, the date 3 January 1698. The word travelled fast. By eight o'clock the curious were beginning to make their way to the church of San Lorenzo in Lucina, just off the Corso – then as now one of the busiest streets in the city. They came along the Corso itself, through the Via Vittoria, along the Via Bocca di Leone and down the Via dei Condotti from the Piazza di Spagna. By midday the crowd inside the church was uncontrollable; at five o'clock, when it began to grow dark, they closed the doors under the portico, guarded by the two ancient stone lions.

The bodies lay side by side on the black and white marble floor before the altar, below Guido Reni's painting of the crucifixion – the man, 69-year-old Pietro Comparini, on the left, his wife Violante, three years his junior, beside him. Early in the morning they had been carried through the chill air, still clad in bloodstained night-clothes, from their house in the Via Vittoria along the almost deserted Corso, over ground tamped hard by the hooves of racing horses, down past the white marble steps of the Palazzo Ruspoli to the triangular Piazza in Lucina and the church of San Lorenzo. Neighbours, who had heard the clamour of the killing, watched silently from doorways. The couple had been stabbed and chopped by their murderers, their heads almost hacked from their bodies; but those who clambered onto chairs, mounted monuments, clung to pillars to get close to the bodies could see that the woman had been most passionately attacked; she had taken so many knife-thrusts to her face that she was almost unrecognisable.

It was said that the Comparini's daughter, Pompilia, only seventeen years old, had been found still alive near the bodies of her parents, and now lay dying in the care of the Augustinian Brothers. Everyone knew that she had recently fled from the house of her husband, Count Guido Franceschini, in Arezzo, and that when he had come to Rome to fetch her back, there had been a scandal – her parents had announced that she was illegitimate, and the husband had branded her an adulteress. The son she had borne not three weeks earlier was said not to be her husband's, but the child of the man with whom she had fled – a priest. Yet someone whose sister had entry to the hospital where Pompilia lay said that she was pious, constantly praying for her murderers, and that Fra Celestino Angelo, who had special care of her, swore that she had all the innocence of the beautiful child she still was.

Meanwhile, at Merluzza, some miles north of Rome, the murderers, physically and emotionally exhausted, lay swaddled in their cloaks before the fire at an inn, their bloodstained knives and daggers still about them – and in the pocket of one of them was the case in which Pietro Comparini had kept his spectacles.

\*     \*     \*

The trial of Count Guido Franceschini and his associates for the murder of his wife Pompilia and her parents was the most sensational of its time. Arguments swelled and eddied around Rome as one half of the population supported a husband's right to murder an adulterous wife, and the other protested Pompilia's innocence. The controversy did not cease even after the final act of the drama, with the Pope's approval of the verdict of the court. It was many years before the crime and its circumstances were forgotten. But, of course, in time they were – for over a century and a half, until the story of the murder and its aftermath surfaced again, not in Italy, but in England.

In September 1846 the poet Robert Browning eloped with Elizabeth Barrett from her father's house in Wimpole Street, London, married her, and whisked her, her maid and her spaniel Flush off to Florence. There the Brownings furnished a flat in the Casa Guida in which they were to spend the whole of their fifteen years of happy marriage. In June 1860, the year before his wife's death, Browning was strolling in the heat of noon in the Piazza Lorenzo and saw on a market stall a 'square old yellow book'. Picking it up, he read the Latin title, which he could translate as:

> A setting-forth of the entire criminal cause against *Guido Franchescini*, nobleman of Arezzo, and his bravos, who were put to death in Rome, 22 February 1698, the first by beheading, the other four by the gallows. Roman murder-case. In which it is disputed whether and when a husband may kill his adulterous wife without incurring the ordinary penalty.

What he had in his hands was the record, in Latin, of a trial for murder which had taken place in Rome 150 years earlier, and on impulse he bought it for one *lira* — eightpence in the English money of the time.

It was clearly fascinating: he walked home with his myopic eyes close to the pages, reading

> from written title-page
> To written index, on, through street and street,
> At the Strozzi, at the Pillar, at the Bridge;
> Till, by the time I stood at home again . . .
> I had mastered the contents, knew the whole truth
> Gathered together, bound up in this book . . .

The book had been put together by a Florentine lawyer, Francesco Cencini, who clearly had a great interest in the case, for he collected together eighteen separate documents, partly in print, partly in manuscript, and bound them in vellum. Presumably the book sat in his library until his death; it then vanished until its reappearance on the bookstall a century and a half later.

Browning did not immediately fasten on the story as material for a poem, and when he showed it to Elizabeth (who was herself a distinguished and admired poet) she took no interest in it at all, so for the time he set it on one side. It seems to have been his wife's death that really sparked off his particular interest in the character of Pompilia; he clearly identified one with the other. When the American novelist Nathaniel Hawthorne called at the Casa Guida in 1858, he described Elizabeth as 'a pale, small person, scarcely embodied at all . . . sweetly disposed towards the human race, though only remotely akin to it', and there is no doubt that as time went on Browning saw his heroine more and more strongly in terms of his late wife. This is no doubt one of the reasons why Pompilia emerges as so much the saint in his treatment of the story – though it is true that the evidence available to him does suggest that she might have been innocent of the charge of adultery.

Browning was to spend eight years reading and re-reading the book, thinking about the characters, refining his view of the story. In 1862 he heard of another source – a manuscript belonging to an acquaintance, Georgina Baker – and acquired it. Two years later he really began work on his poem, devising its shape and construction while on holiday in the spa town of Cambo at the foot of the Pyrenees. It was published in 1868, and won immediate and enormous fame.

*The Ring and the Book* was a success not only because of Browning's much-admired technical skill, but because of the drama of the story (even if it was a touch earthy for Victorian taste) and in particular because of the perceived perfection of its heroine – an innocent, saintly young girl accused of a crime she did not commit. It was a portrait that immediately appealed to the readers of the time, particularly perhaps the women readers. Pompilia's innocence was taken for granted by him and by them – and was not questioned for many years. Indeed, the poem's glory had begun to fade, and it was beginning to become one of the unread classics of nineteenth-century literature. Then new evidence surfaced.

Browning's view of Pompilia was perfectly understandable; the documents in *The Old Yellow Book* present both sides of the case, but are certainly tilted towards the suggestion that Guido was mistaken in assuming that his wife had betrayed him. However, in 1940 an American scholar, Beatrice Corrigan – fortunately a student and admirer of Browning's work – while working in the Biblioteca del Comune in Cortona came across a manuscript almost twice the size of the *Yellow Book*, which she saw to her excitement consisted of documents dealing with (as its title announced) the 'Deplorable and impious homicide committed in Rome by Guido son of the late Tomaso Franceschini and 4 other Companions on the Persons of Pietro Comparini and Violante Peruzzo Spouses and Francesca Pompilia believed the daughter of the same . . .' The documents contained a great deal of evidence which Browning's source did not – and a lot of that evidence threw new light on the personality and character of Pompilia. It does not quite close the case, but it certainly strongly suggests that she was not necessarily the saint Browning took her for.

Following the case from its tawdry beginnings to its sordid climax and its bloody end is fascinating, but fleshing out the story has its difficulties. Seventeenth-century Italy is one of the least well-documented periods of history. Certainly there are travellers' tales, letters, documents – such as those in the *Yellow Book* and the Cortona Codex – but the social life of the time, and certainly the legal processes, are often in deep shadow. We know little, for instance, about just what it was like to be in a Roman courtroom in the 1690s. How did the lawyers conduct themselves? Was there a real cut-and-thrust of debate or, as the records suggest, simply very long, uninterrupted legal arguments? Were members of the public admitted? – very probably not. Were the accused men examined before the court, and able to expand on or deny the statements they had been forced to make under torture? It seems unlikely. Then there are the sources so liberally quoted for precedence by the defence and prosecution lawyers: who were Nellus a San Geminiano, Brunus de Perilis, Vulpellus and Gracchus and Matarazzus? Their treatises, often in manuscript, lie rotting on the shelves of ancient libraries, their names often only names even to authorities such as Judge John Marshall Gest, who wrote the only modern gloss on the available records of the case.

More important from the point of view of the story is the fact that we cannot see the characters clearly. There is a sketch of the miserable Count, made as he went on his way to his execution, and this seems to bear out Browning's description of him (which is not surprising, since the sketch was tipped into his *Yellow Book*). But we have only a cursory hint of Pompilia's beauty, and we can only guess (perhaps for the sake of the drama, hope) that her supposed lover, Giuseppe Caponsacchi, was handsome, and that the Count's accomplices were uncouth ruffians.

This leaves a writer hovering over a choice between presenting characters in their bare bones or dressed in imagined clothes. The middle ground is marshy and full of the possibility of disaster. I hope that where I have made assumptions they are not too outrageous, that where I have guessed it has not been with too much impertinence; I have tried to do both on reasonable grounds, but in many cases (that, for instance, of Pompilia's child, of whom we know nothing) the reader's guess will be as good as mine.

Given the fact that what we have is too often a scaffolding rather than a building, this is still a story which engages the emotions: the desperation of a child sold into marriage with a man old enough to be her father calls clearly to us – and it needs little imagination to understand the fatal wound inflicted on Guido's pride when his wife deserted him, or the virtual frenzy with which so many men of his class flew to his defence; their own pride was at risk, their own wives might catch the contagion. Caponsacchi, Pompilia's lover, is perfectly recognisable as a type – a handsome ne'er-do-well with too much time on his hands, persuaded against what little judgement he had into an elopement, and absconding the moment the going got tough.

It is rare for a set of characters to emerge clearly from seventeenth-century Italy; though at first those of Pompilia's story seem almost lay figures, as the drama progresses we can identify with most of them – even, perhaps, with the young bravos and their game to beat up an errant wife, inveigled by an older ruffian into a fatal adventure. No wonder the drama attracted Browning. The Cortona Codex has fleshed his rather bald narrative out into something far more complex, human and real to us.

The mystery lies, as it did from the moment of the trial, in the character of Pompilia. Guido's guilt was obvious, and what suspense there was about his fate lay only in his hesitation to avenge himself on his wife the moment he discovered her infidelity. Had he killed her immediately, would he still have been beheaded? That depended on the court's view of Pompilia's character – and about that there is still some doubt.

*O N E*

# The Marriage of a Most Beloved Daughter

*How very different a lot is mine*
*From any other woman's in the world.*
*The reason must be, 'twas by step and step*
*It got to grow so terrible and strange:*
*These strange woes stole on tiptoe, as it were . . .*

Pietro Comparini lived in Rome with his wife Violante in a house opposite the Via dei Greci, near the corner of the Via Vittoria and the Strada Paolina (now the Via del Babuino), just off the Corso. At the end of the seventeenth century, the Via Vittoria was a narrow, rather mean street in a middle-class district. One travel writer of the period, Salvatore Silvagni, called it 'as squalid a street as there was in Rome', though the houses had large gardens at their backs, and here and there stood a fine palace or small mansion. In the city, as in other European cities, the poor, the middle class and the rich lived cheek by jowl, and the former had to put up with the stench and mess distributed about the streets by the latter (who used the roadways not only as a market-place but also as a latrine).

The Corso was a fine thoroughfare distinguished by noble palaces such as the Palazzo Aldobrandini; but the area as a whole was not particularly elegant. Silvagni described it just after the Comparini's time:

> The streets were without names, the houses without numbers, the roofs without gutters and the shop windows without glass. There were no foot pavements, no lamps, no names over the tradespeople's premises . . . There were huge open drains full of filth and nastiness of every kind running down the middle of most of the streets, the Corso included. As an exception to the general rule, the Corso had a sidewalk for foot passengers raised above the roadway all along it.

Most houses were two storeys high, the eaves of their red-tiled roofs hanging over the street to give shade to the customers visiting the shops on the ground floor, though the streets were narrow enough to be in shade for much of the day. The street-scene must have been very little different from that of the days of Imperial Rome, and perhaps the best way of visualising it is to think of the remains of Italy's ancient cities – even at the end of the eighteenth century men still drank in bars which looked much the same as those of Pompeii, and women still brushed out rooms no more elaborate than those of Herculaneum.

The Comparini themselves were middle class. Francesco, the father of Pietro, had died in 1645, leaving his property entailed under what was called a *fedecommesso* – a device much used by Romans of the time to tie up estates until a male heir was born, or at least a daughter who might marry and then succeed. Pietro inherited two houses in Rome, one in the Piazza Lombarda with a coach-house attached, and one in which he lived, consisting of a shop on the ground floor looking onto the street, a large pair of scissors hanging over the door to advertise the fact that it was let to a tailor, and two floors above in which he and his wife lived. He also owned another shop behind his house, on the Orti di Napoli (now part of the Via Margutta) which he rented to a glass-blower, whose furnace glowed, night and day.

A dark passage led from the street at the side of the tailor's shop to the Comparini's front door, and an even darker stone staircase mounted to the first floor where there was a kitchen, living-room and one bedroom; up another set of stairs, a drawing-room and two bedrooms. Though many houses in the area were barely furnished, the Comparini's rooms had touches of luxury – visitors admired a harpsichord covered with yellow leather, and a gilded four-poster in the main bedroom. Those visitors included some of moderate distinction: Signora Comparini's oldest friend was the wife of the steward of Benedetto Maidalchini, the

Grand Prior of Rome and a great-nephew of Pope Innocent X. The steward of such a man was himself of considerable importance.

Pietro must have seemed wealthy – he owned property, lived well, kept two servants, and gave the impression of having money. Indeed, he could not be described as poor: his father had left some bonds worth between 10,000 and 12,000 *scudi* (between £212,000 and £254,000 in today's money). The problem was that he could not get at the capital, and most of the interest had immediately to be re-invested. This was probably fortunate, for he was constitutionally lazy. He had certain skills – he was addressed as *dottore* in official documents, so he had been to a university – but those skills were unexercised. He loved good food and good wine, but was not especially fond of work, and spent far too much time lazing about in local taverns. Any money on which he could lay his hands was spent on comfortable living and good wine. He and his wife lived well, their meals rather more elaborate than their poorer neighbours': for dinner, broth, boiled beef or fritters, roast fowl, fresh or dried fish on Fridays, eggs, salad vegetables and fruit.

Violante Peruzzi, whom Pietro had married in 1666 when he was thirty-seven and she was thirty-four, was of the same class as himself, and had brought a small dowry with her. One gets the impression that the chief reason for Pietro's marriage was to get a child; there is no evidence that his love for his wife was overwhelming. But though she fell pregnant several times, she always miscarried in the fifth month, and by the time Pietro was fifty-two and his wife was forty-nine he had given up hope of a child, and was surprised when Violante, at such an advanced age, declared herself pregnant. His pleasure was increased when his wife pointed out that the child, if they were fortunate enough to have a daughter, might prove a passport to a comfortable old age if they could marry her off to a wealthy suitor. This was, of course, true; and even if they had a son, he could be put to work and would surely prove an insurance against destitution. However, a daughter might be most profitable – marrying money brought safety; merely working for it was a less certain business.

Violante's pregnancy was an easy one. Perhaps for fear of disappointing him if things went badly, she did not tell Pietro of the possible birth until the baby was almost due, and by the time she began to show the uncommonly hot summer weather was exhausting for her. She kept her husband at bay, insisting on separate bedrooms – she was sure (she said) that her previous miscarriages had happened because they had made love while she was pregnant. He heard her retching with morning sickness, and when her term had nearly come she lost her appetite, eating only an egg or two at mealtimes.

One afternoon she sent him out on an errand, knowing perfectly well that he would end up at some tavern. A little later she called downstairs to Giovanna Boba, the tailor's wife, and when Giovanna hobbled upstairs (she had hurt her knee in a fall) she found the midwife, Angela Biondi, already there. She was asked to climb onto the gilded four-poster bed behind Violante and support her shoulders. After only a minute or so, with surprising speed and ease, a handsome baby was delivered, and when Pietro had been found and hurried home he was greeted by the smell of a roasting ceremonial chicken and the sight of a healthily squalling baby girl being bathed in a huge copper basin. Violante stayed abed for a week, visited by congratulatory friends, and the baby was put out to a series of wet-nurses (for Violante's breasts were obstinately dry).

So Francesca Camilla Vittoria Angela Pompilia was born on 17 July 1680, and six days later specially hired coaches took her parents, her godmother Barbara Caporossi, who lived across the street, her godfather Giovan Battista Barberij and some other friends the short step from the Comparini's house to San Lorenzo in Lucina for her baptism by the curate, Bartolomeo Mini. The church, which in a few years was to see the bloody exhibition of the bodies of the parents, was not one of the most fashionable in the city, but it was certainly one of the oldest, and was the family's parish church. Handsome enough, it had been re-fashioned some thirty years previously by the architect Cosimo Fanzago, who had partly demolished the old twelfth-century building, leaving the campanile and the four-square porch with the two lions that still guard it. Three major paintings, then as now, looked down on the worshippers – the crucifixion over the altar, a St Charles by the Venetian Carlo Saraceni and a St Francis by the Frenchman Simon Vouet.

Her parents were careful about Pompilia's nursing, which went on for some time: most children were suckled for at least two years, some – possibly including Pompilia – until they went to school. Because Violante had no milk (she told Pietro that she had reacted badly to some liquid with which the midwife had bathed her breasts), the child was nursed first by Signora Boba; but then the latter's eight-month-old son fell ill, and Violante got worried and gave Pompilia to a wet-nurse called Maddalena, who nursed her for ten months on payment of two *scudi* a month (about £10 a week). Then there was more trouble: the second wet-nurse's own child fell ill and died, and her milk dried up, so Pompilia was sent to another Maddalena – until she was found to be giving some of her milk to her own baby. Once again they had to renew the search, and this time settled on a dressmaker – a widow called Agnese Santa Olivieri, who nursed the child for four months while living in the Comparini's house. Then she left for 'a better situation'. Finally, Pietro and Violante settled on Petronilla, their servant Domenico's wife, who was Pompilia's last nurse.

It was easy to spoil Pompilia, for everyone noticed her beauty, her aquiline nose, her huge black eyes – indeed, she grew more beautiful as she approached puberty. Her mother sometimes seemed a little cool towards her – curiously, the neighbours thought, for an elderly mother with a young daughter was usually passionately fond – but she was thoroughly spoiled by her indulgent father. As soon as she could walk they were to be seen hand in hand in the streets near the house. When she was four, she was sent to a school run by a young woman called Margherita, a few doors along the Via Babuino. The mistress called for her every day, and she stayed until she was eight, learning to read and write tolerably well. Pompilia was fortunate in being kept at home; many daughters were sent to convents between the age of seven or eight and their marriage, and emerged 'broken-spirited and ignorant of everything in the world'.

During the 1670s and 1680s financial problems made life increasingly difficult for the Comparini. The relatively small income that Pietro was allowed from the interest on his bonds was insufficient for anything but a moderately comfortable life, and some of the interest-bearing bonds had been handed over to a creditor. Moreover, his resources were continually drained by a number of obscure lawsuits, and by 'misfortunes' of one kind or another – he was several times arrested for debt. In 1685 Pope Innocent XI called in most of his bonds at a very low price, which further diminished Pietro's fortune. He looked forward with keen anticipation to the time when Pompilia would reach marriageable age and some relief would be in sight. He was, at least in theory, no less averse than his wife to coupling her with the highest bidder.

She was certainly, to put it coarsely, a desirable property. Violante, though no paragon, had taken care that her daughter should be as respectable as she was beautiful. There was a strict regime for bringing up middle-class Italian girls which had scarcely altered since the days of Imperial Rome, and Violante applied it vigorously. Only as very young children were girls allowed to play freely in the streets or gardens. The moment they approached adolescence, they were kept at home except when accompanied by their mother or a responsible servant – harm might come to them if they were let out alone to go shopping or deliver a message. It was undesirable even to allow them near an open door or a window lest they show themselves off and flirt with passers-by. An additional reason for keeping girls at home was the general lawlessness of the city. Rome was a place in which no woman could feel safe after dark for danger of the footpads and ranging rapists who hid in the squalid alleys and among the ramshackle hovels that were thrown up even in the most handsome *piazze*. So when Pompilia went out, she was accompanied by her mother, even if she merely walked up to the top of the nearby Pincian hill for fresh vegetables from the kitchen garden tilled by the monks of Santa Maria del Popolo.

Though Pompilia was literate, she was not encouraged to read – books could be dangerous. Evil thoughts were always ready to jump from the page into unoccupied, agile young minds. So girls, especially adolescent girls, were to be kept busy with housework, needlework, 'womanly' occupations. The four necessary virtues were to be encouraged – modesty, piety, chastity and beauty; the last two invariably paired, for to possess a daughter who had beauty without chastity was (as the moralist and essayist Nicolò Vito di Gozze had put it in a celebrated open letter to parents) like adorning a pig with inestimable jewels.

Like many only children, especially those not encouraged to mix with their contemporaries, Pompilia developed a highly active imagination and a tendency to fantasise, especially, perhaps, about men – an unknown quantity to a girl whose only view of them was from a distance. She must have wondered, on the rare occasions when she could look from her window into the busy street and watch the passers-by, how she could possibly meet her prince. Soon enough, she was to be introduced to him.

In the autumn of 1693, when Pompilia was thirteen, Count Guido Franceschini, a 35-year-old nobleman from an aristocratic family of the Tuscan walled city of Arezzo, just over a hundred miles north of Rome, was in the holy city visiting his elder brother, the Abate Paolo. The Franceschini had fallen on hard times. In 1681, their father Tomaso had died intestate, leaving five indigent children – a daughter, Porzia, and four sons, Paolo, Girolamo, Guido and Antonio Maria. The financial situation was so desperate that the two younger sons, Guido and Antonio Maria, actually repudiated their inheritance in order to evade the claims of the family's creditors.

Tomaso's widow, Beatrice (who had been born of the dei Romani family, considerably more aristocratic than the Franceschini), was able to secure a good match for Porzia, who married Canon Giovanni Battista Conti, an Arezzan nobleman, the younger brother of Count Aldobrandi, whose fine *palazzo* dignified the city. The family had a tradition of church service, and all four brothers took holy orders, after which Girolamo and Antonia Maria were able to secure benefices in the town. Paolo went to Rome in 1683 armed with an introduction from his mother to her acquaintance Cardinal Chigi, whose influence got him the position of secretary to Cardinal Lauria, one of the most distinguished churchmen in the holy city, and a prime candidate for the papacy. Paolo speedily impressed the Cardinal with his abilities, and within a few years was established as an important member of Lauria's household, had become moderately wealthy, and was the owner of a house in the city and a profitable vineyard at Ponte Milvio, a hamlet two miles outside Rome, where he also had a small villa (one or two were scattered in what was otherwise a miserable semi-suburb with wretched houses and dirty inns used by peasants).

Guido also came to Rome and succeeded in becoming secretary to a cardinal – in his case, to Cardinal Nerli, formerly Archbishop of Florence and Papal Nuncio in Paris. But Guido lacked his brother's intelligence and was dismissed after only a few months' service. He had only taken minor orders and was therefore free to marry – Italian men of fairly large families often took this precaution, in order that the line should not die out. Guido decided to repair his fortunes and those of his house by marrying an heiress. His name – the name of the Franceschini family – was about his only advantage. In person, he was unattractive – thin and pale, with a beaky nose, and a shaggy black beard – but he was, after all, a nobleman and a man of property (he boasted continually of his birth and his estate). Abate Paolo's reputation also shed some lustre. In fact, Guido scarcely had enough money on which to live. Anyone might have guessed at this, for rather than staying in comfortable lodgings, he lived in a mean set of rooms in the Piazza Colonna owned by a woman whose reputation was less than pristine.

One day he called at the shop of a wig-maker, Antonia Scarduelli, to pick up a wig he had ordered. Was it for his wife, Signora Scarduelli enquired? No, for an acquaintance in Florence, he replied. He had no wife. But, he confided, he was not against acquiring one, provided her family could offer a good dowry of, say, 8,000 or 10,000 *scudi* – £170,000 to £212,000. He would, of course, be properly grateful to Signora Scarduelli should she be able to introduce him to a suitable candidate. Though Guido completed his commission to buy the wig, he returned again and again to the shop, ostensibly for a general gossip, but clearly curious whether Antonia had heard of a candidate who might make a suitable wife. Her daughter Ursula happened to know the Marchesa Panthasilea Capozzi, who lived in the Via de'Crociferi, and promised to ask her. The Marchesa said she would tell her servants and pass on any news of possible occupants for the position of Countess of the Franceschini family.

One of the Marchesa's servants, Cecilia, soon reported a possibility. There was a family called

Comparini who had a daughter of marriageable age, and could confidently be expected to provide a suitably generous dowry (the rumour was that Pietro was a miser, and had more money than appeared to be the case). Cecilia had known Violante since before her marriage, and while her husband could not be said to be distinguished, she knew theirs was a respectable family. Having talked to Cecilia and confirmed the story, as far as it could be confirmed, Antonia pointed the couple out to Guido and enthusiastically commended Pompilia – a daughter both beautiful and young – as a possible bride. Guido was averse neither to beauty nor to youth – indeed the fact that Pompilia was twenty-two years his junior was an advantage rather than an obstacle. He ought, however, to see a note of Signor Comparini's property, he said; the hairdresser replied that it was surely for him to write down an account of his own circumstances first.

Next day he gave her a folded sheet of paper – a list of all his property. It began with a lie – Guido put himself down as thirty, when he was really thirty-five. He and his brothers owned 'a very comfortable house in which they live, superior to that of many noblemen and inferior to that of none', which was worth some 3,000 *scudi* (£63,300 in the year 2000). There were two more houses, rented for a total of 29 *scudi* (£614) a year, and a farm at Vitiano, two miles outside Arezzo, which every year brought in about 2,000 *scudi* (£42,400) in oil, wheat, wine, vegetables and fruit, and had attached to it an elegant farmhouse ideal for a summer break from the claustrophobia of the town, and a pleasant garden in which to entertain friends while doves circled over the two neat little dovecotes. Apart from this property, the family also owned another farm, a vineyard, chestnut woods and an olive grove; then there was an income from livestock and from 'certain liquid assets' and 'certain agricultural assets.'

Guido went on to list his relatives: his elder brother Paolo was forty-two (actually, forty-three), and was in the service of Cardinal Lauria – but he also enjoyed a benefice in Arezzo which brought him in 40 *scudi* (£848) a year, and another in the country which added another 80 *scudi* (£1,696). The second brother, Girolamo, was thirty-five (actually thirty-nine), and was a canon of the cathedral at Arezzo at 80 *scudi* a year, with three additional benefices bringing in a total of 62 *scudi* (£1,314) a year. Finally, there was Antonio Maria, aged twenty-eight, who had also been a canon of the cathedral, but had resigned his place to Canon Conti, Guido's sister's husband, and gone to live in his own parish outside the city, where his income was 500 *scudi* (£10,600) a year, though an additional 30 (£636) came in from a distant benefice in another county.

Perhaps he should also say, Guido concluded, that his family was engaged in a number of lawsuits over entailed property and for the recovery of money owed them, which, when the verdicts went in the Franceschini's favour (as they certainly would), would bring in almost 5,000 *scudi* (£106,600). They lived in the style to be expected of such a family: their house in Arezzo was comfortably, even luxuriously, furnished, with fine works of art – everything fit for a gentleman and a gentleman's wife. He would, of course, engage whatever servants his wife might require.

A lot of this was smoke in the wind, but Pompilia's mother was not to know that. She was thoroughly impressed, and Antonia arranged a meeting at the house of the Marchesa Capozzi between Violante, Guido and Abate Paolo. The brothers wooed Violante with compliments and presents, impressing her with the graciousness of their condescension, and persuading her that their family was sufficiently wealthy to be able to keep not only her child but also herself and Pietro in comfort for the rest of their lives. She and the two brothers reached an immediate agreement: she would persuade her husband to consult Guido about a marriage contract.

The prospect of a rich dowry (Antonia was quite clear about the family's wealth) far outweighed any doubts Guido might have had about the difference between his rank as a nobleman (however penurious) and that of Pompilia's family, while her daughter's future as a countess appealed to Violante – though in general, it was thought not only improper but unwise to marry out of your class, for if a husband was superior to his wife he would tend to treat her like a child, while if he was of a lower class than her, she would disdain him and treat him like a servant.

Though Pietro had always hoped that Pompilia would marry money, when it came to it and he was told that he was expected to consult an unknown 'foreigner' (Arezzo was foreign territory to a Roman) about a possible marriage with his much-loved daughter, he was far from happy. The more he saw of Guido Franceschini, the less happy he became. He made discreet enquiries of an acquaintance whose business took him to Arezzo and found that his misgivings seemed to be justified: the family was by no means as wealthy as the brothers had claimed. Even the relatively small annual income of 1,200 *scudi* – only just over £25,540 at today's valuation – claimed by the suitor was a fiction. Moreover, the house to which it was proposed he should carry his bride did not belong to him, but to his mother and elder brothers.

Pietro kept from Guido the fact that he had been looking into the Franceschini's circumstances – the man was already displaying signs of a short temper, and it would be best to be sure of the ground before tackling him about his financial situation. Privately, he told Violante that, whatever the consequences, he was not prepared to fulfil the contract, and began making excuses: Pompilia was too young, too ill-informed, too ignorant to be married to a nobleman. However, the nagging of his wife and the ostentatious charm of Guido and Paolo persuaded him, against his better judgement, to enter into negotiations. The fact that Pompilia's marriage would release funds with which he could buy off some of his creditors was certainly a factor in its favour. And, after all, the suitor was a nobleman.

Aware that Pietro was less than entirely enthusiastic, Guido brought in his brother, the Abate, and Paolo engaged the help of his employer, the Cardinal, to assure Pietro of the respectability and financial status of the Franceschini family. In the end, without being greatly placated, Pietro was persuaded to give his reluctant consent to the marriage and he signed two marriage contracts. The first ceded to Guido the administration of Pietro's two houses (including the income from them) and three of his bonds, on condition that the Count agree that the Comparini family should all live with him at Arezzo, 'for their greater quiet and comfort and for the affection that they bear to their most beloved daughter'. The second marriage contract assigned twenty-four of Pietro's bonds to the Count, reserving ten for his own use, and three more which had been pledged and awaited redemption. The income from Pietro's thirteen reserved bonds was to be for Pompilia, together with half of his capital when and if that became available. The total dowry amounted to about 8,000 *scudi* (about

£169,600 in today's money); this was generous for its time. Though Pietro took the precaution, with one excuse or the other, of handing over only about a quarter of it in cash, it left him with very little disposable income.

Guido agreed to carry Pompilia and her parents to Arezzo, where they were to live with him, completely provided for, 'not only with food but with clothing and with service'. His family was to show 'every other affectionate regard for Signori Pietro and Violante as long as they continued to live in his parental house'. Guido was to allow 20 *scudi* a year – £424 – in cash to Pietro and Violante, which he would pay them as pocket money. If Pietro died, he was to continue to provide for Violante, and pay her the annuity. If both Pietro and Violante should die, the money would go to Pompilia. If 'through some unforeseen contingency' the Comparini ever wanted to return to Rome, Guido was obliged to move them back there at his own expense. The contract was signed on 24 June 1693 by Pietro, Violante, Pompilia, Guido, Paolo and two witnesses – Abate Cosetti and Luca Santoli of Arezzo.

Guido clearly profited more from this arrangement than the Comparini could. He was, nominally at any rate, in possession of the greater part of Pietro's property, and all he had to do in return (in addition to the normal duties of a husband) was give Pompilia's parents a home for the rest of their lives. What the arrangement did not take into consideration, of course, was the frequent tension that arises between a wife's parents and her in-laws – particularly between the two mothers – and the fact that neither Guido nor Pietro were men who would willingly hand over more money to the other than was absolutely necessary, and, if possible, not even that.

But all had been settled reasonably amicably, and on 6 September 1693, Guido and Pompilia went to San Lorenzo's in the heaviest rainstorm Rome had seen for many years and were married. Later, some people claimed that the marriage had been performed secretly for fear that Pietro would forbid the banns, but no; he sat, ill-tempered and grudging, while those banns were read on three of the Sundays in July, and, reconciled to the occasion, endured – not in a much better temper – the marriage ceremony itself. Abate Paolo, who had seen to the detail of the arrangements between the two families, was absent – on that very day his employer, Cardinal Lauria, died, and he now lacked employment.

The marriage of a thirteen-year-old child to a man twenty-two years older than her doubtless caused some comment in the families who knew the Comparini. It was a rather surprising event. Medieval girls often wed almost before they reached puberty, but by the end of the seventeenth century daughters married at about twenty-two or twenty-three on average, while sons were usually between twenty-four and twenty-six. Generally, and for economic reasons, the poorer the family, the older the bride and groom. By the 1690s there was a great deal more free choice for young people. Nevertheless, where marriages were arranged, bride and groom could be of almost any age, and the age gap between them was equally variable. Among the aristocracy – and not only in Italy – there were three main considerations where the marriage of a child was concerned: the provision of an heir, rank and money. Children often failed to survive infancy, and so a somewhat older man would look for a wife young and vigorous enough to bear several children, in the hope that at least one would live long enough to continue the line. Sometimes the wives were, indeed, what we would call children. In general, while it was considered unwise for girls under sixteen to marry, as that could lead to difficult pregnancies and deformed children, a young woman would probably have an easier pregnancy and bear more healthy children than an older one. Moreover, an older woman might well have ideas of her own, and be difficult to control. As Nicolò Gozze put it, you can't get an old ox to plough. If such considerations did not weigh as heavily with Guido as the dowry, they were certainly among Pompilia's additional attractions.

For a few weeks after the wedding Guido and his bride stayed in Rome, presumably with her parents. The groom made no attempt to consummate the marriage, and it was agreed that the couple would sleep together only when they and Pompilia's parents had travelled to Arezzo, met Guido's mother and settled into their home. In happy anticipation of a prolonged stay in a comfortable, possibly even luxurious, noble family mansion, Pietro and Violante accompanied their daughter and her husband on the dusty and exhausting hundred-mile journey to Arezzo, where they were greeted by Signora Beatrice Franceschini (or Beatrice dei Romani, as she often styled herself, retaining her more distinguished maiden name) and Canon Girolamo Franceschini, Guido's second brother. Antonio Maria, the youngest, had left home.

Arezzo was no backwater and at first sight the family was impressed. The city had a long and distinguished history. It had been one of the most noteworthy of the twelve cities of the Etruscans, and later became an important Roman stronghold, guarding the Appennine passes and dominating the upper and middle valleys of the Arno (the upper course of the Tiber), the Valdichiana and the road south to Rome. The monumental ruins of the Roman amphitheatre still dominated the town, and craftsmen still worked to produce the red-glazed vases or *corallini* which they had sold for centuries throughout the Western world.

In 1535 Arezzo had, with the rest of Tuscany, been incorporated into the Medici Grand Duchy, and the

Medici fortress stood stolidly above the town, cheek by jowl with the modest thirteenth-century Gothic Duomo and the Palazzo Comunale, from which the main street, the Corso, ran down past the Church of Santa Maria della Pieve to the San Spirito Gate, by which the travellers entered the city. Out from the Corso, small paved streets scarcely more than alleys ran in convoluted zigzags towards the walls of the city.

The parents-in-law were received politely enough, but without warmth; and the Franceschini *palazzo*, though it was impressively situated near the Piazza Grande with its medieval houses and towers, was far from what they expected. The furnishings were threadbare and uncomfortable, the very fabric of the house itself had clearly been deteriorating for years, and the hospitality offered to them on their first night was to say the least ungenerous. The table was meanly set, with the minimum of food and wine, and the room to which they were conducted was bitterly cold and without a fire.

Pietro lost no time in going into the town and finding the most agreeable taverns where, apart from good wine, he found a lot of gossip and some new facts about the Franceschini – for instance, the family was not as noble as Guido had claimed. (Later, Chancellor Bernardino Balsamini, an expert in the families of Arezzo, was to testify that 'in an official book of tax duties of the said city . . . it is apparent that among the eight ranks of which the gentility of Arezzo is composed, beginning with the Gondfaloniere, the Franceschini family enjoys the second rank.')

From the very first the two families were at each other's throats. Only five months after the marriage letters from Arezzo were already beginning to worry Paolo in Rome. On 6 February 1694, the Abate was writing to advise Pietro that he really must moderate his and his wife's behaviour towards Beatrice: unless they showed a little restraint, he could not say what might not happen.

Beatrice, the only real aristocrat in the house, considered that Guido had married so far beneath him as to make his wife's family almost invisible. Paolo was soon writing continually to Violante in answer to complaints about the Franceschini's treatment of their in-laws, reminding her that he and she had a joint responsibility, as the original negotiators of the marriage, to see that the relationship between the families worked – she, Violante, by not complaining so much about negligible details of life at Arezzo, and Paolo by using his influence to persuade both parties to 'peace and love'.

There was not much chance of that. Any hope that things might get better was speedily dispersed. Two mothers-in-law in the same house traditionally make for trouble, and when they are both used to having their own way, things are apt to go from bad to worse.

They did – the food, in particular. In the first place, there was not a great deal of it. The usual joint was two pounds of beef, which was made to last the family for seven days. On at least one occasion a suckling lamb was also made to last for a week, the head divided up and served on three successive days as a starter, the lights and intestines making the main course on two days. If the supply of meat ran out, as it often did, the table bore only vegetable soup, a little salted fish, sometimes boiled chestnuts. More often than not, when there was beef, it was undercooked and so tough that the elderly Pietro could not chew it and had to live mostly on stale black bread and a little cheese. One flask containing a pint of well-watered wine was put on the table to serve five people.

Neither Pietro nor Violante were of the temperament to put up with such conditions without bitter complaint, and Pietro in particular had a cutting tongue when he cared to use it; Violante began to treat the entire Franceschini family with a haughty disdain, which only made Beatrice more determined to make her guests as uncomfortable as possible. She was sixty-two years old and unused to having her authority questioned (her only daughter, Porzia, had been delighted to marry into the Aldobrandini family and get away from her). In a very short time she succeeded in making her guests' lives thoroughly miserable. Her pride became even more intolerable when, Cardinal

Lauria having died, Paolo was appointed to the prestigious position of Secretary in Rome of the Religious Order of the Knights of St John of Malta, whose headquarters were in a handsome building with a delightful cloister and a charming fountain in the Via Condotti, not far from the Via Vittoria.

The Comparini's discomfort was observed by one of Signora Franceschini's servants, one Angelica Batista, who was recruited from the nearby village of Castelluccio just after Guido's wedding party arrived. Among the instructions given to Angelica by her employer was the injunction to have nothing whatsoever to do with 'the old people' – Pompilia's parents. Should either of them call for attention, she should ignore the summons until she was able to ask Beatrice's permission to answer it. The young country girl needed the position, but found these conditions difficult – how could one ignore the plight of an elderly woman who spent most of her day in an icy chamber, so 'stiff with cold' that she continually wept? On one occasion Angelica took a shovel of hot coals from her own fire and carried it to the Comparini's room, though Violante refused to accept it lest Beatrice should discover the maid's duplicity and dismiss her. The girl insisted, and her kindness became a nightly habit – until one evening Beatrice encountered her with her shovel of coals, snatched it from her hands and threatened instant dismissal.

The bitter chill of the house, uncomfortable in summer, was insufferable in winter, and was a continual problem for the Comparini. Taken ill one evening in December after a punishing altercation with Guido, Violante went to her room and collapsed. Pompilia, unable to rouse her, panicked and demanded a doctor. Nonsense, her husband replied; Angelica could care for her. The maid unlaced the unconscious woman's bodice and with the help of vinegar and water brought her round. She then went to lay a fire but was told by Beatrice that warm ashes from the fire downstairs would be perfectly adequate. By the time the maid had carried them up the narrow stone staircase to the bedroom, they were too cold to do any good, and by the time she and Pompilia had undressed Violante and got her into bed, her limbs were icy cold. When Angelica suggested she should make some hot gruel, her mistress forbade it; and when the kindly maid began to weep in sympathy with the sick elderly guest, Beatrice ironically offered her coarse sackcloth with which to wipe her eyes.

Pompilia's mother was not the only one to suffer. Her father, who badly missed the companionship of the Roman taverns, took to sneaking out regularly for a drink and company more congenial than that of the Franceschini's friends, whom he found snobbish, dull and boring. Guido, in particular, was infuriated when he discovered that Pietro had been seen in common drinking-houses, consorting with common people. No Franceschini would have been seen dead in a tavern. This disreputable behaviour by a house guest had to be curbed. On one occasion when Pietro returned after dark, he found the street door locked, and no one would answer it. He eventually managed to attract his wife's attention, and she came downstairs to let him in. As she stepped out of the doorway, perhaps to offer an arm to a man a little the worse for liquor, someone slid from the shadows and slammed the door behind her. She was forced to ask a neighbour for a bed, and he slept rough at an inn. When they complained next morning, there was a violent quarrel.

On another evening, hearing Pietro knock, Angelica took a torch to light his way up the treacherous stone staircase (where, a while ago, he had fallen, bruising himself so badly that he was confined to bed). Guido, intercepting her, snatched the light from her hands, telling her that if she carried on with such unwarranted attentions he would pitch her out of the window. Fearing another fall, the old man was reduced to crawling up the stairs on all fours. On a further occasion when Violante went to find her husband, who had again been locked out, both of them were refused entry, and appealed both to the Governor, Senator Vincenzo Marzi-Medici, and to Bishop Marchetti, who – friends of the Franceschini – intervened to secure an uneasy and brief peace.

The Comparini's discomfort continued for four months: not only were the elderly couple continually distressed by the cold, but the food they were served was insufficient to energise their bodies and keep them warm. Pompilia witnessed their wretchedness, but at thirteen lacked the self-confidence to protest, while by now she had had to come to terms with the sexual demands of an older husband eager to produce a son, and with his disappointment when she did not immediately conceive.

Nor did Paolo succeed in producing the right sort of oil to smooth the troubled waters. He was fully aware of the bitterness and even hatred that now separated the two parties, and when Violante suggested he should transfer himself from Rome to Arezzo in order to be able to make a more immediate contribution to promoting a cessation of hostilities, he was horrified, though he put his horror into fairly polite terms: he was 'reluctant to engage myself to live in one household with you and Signor Pietro, since I should not want to lose that tranquillity and peace that I desire for others, and that by God's grace I have enjoyed until now. Because I am convinced that from morning until evening and at every moment you would deafen me with chatter and complaints.'

Paolo did make an attempt to be even-handed. He told Pietro (in a letter of 4 March 1694) that he was not really interested in hearing who was right and who was wrong in their disputes – he blamed both parties for not being able to live together in peace, or even just to tolerate each other for the sake of avoiding scandal. 'I shudder to think,' he wrote, 'of the mockery that must be going on in that native city of mine, and perhaps in Rome among those who have news of it . . .'

Eventually, enough was enough. The Comparini decided to leave Arezzo and return to Rome. Learning that Beatrice had given Angelica notice, they asked a favour as the family sat at their sparse evening meal. Would Beatrice keep the girl on for another week or ten days? Then the couple would take her back with them as their servant. There was a silence. Then Guido got up from the table, walked around to where Angelica stood, and struck her twice in the face. His brother Girolamo gave her a kick for good measure, and finally Beatrice also struck the girl and told her to leave the house immediately. The Comparini and Pompilia sat speechless, unable to intervene. When Violante asked where Beatrice expected the poor girl to go, the Signora called her a slut, and told her that she could get out too.

Violante left the room and went to her chamber, followed by the Canon, who drew his sword, entered the room after her and locked the door behind him. Pompilia began to cry as her father, trembling, stood helplessly by. Angelica, frightened out of her wits, ran from the house, and went back to her village.

Pietro now realised that the small store of *scudi* he had brought with him to Arezzo had vanished – some given to Beatrice, at her insistence, to pay for the miserable, inadequate meals, some spent on consolatory drafts of wine at nearby taverns. He reminded Guido that under the terms of the marriage contract he had agreed to pay for his parents-in-law to return to Rome should they wish to do so. His only reward was a sneer. He then went to Pompilia's room and pocketed a number of trinkets of hers which he hoped to be able to sell to some local jeweller. Guido, discovering this, appealed to his friend the Governor, claiming that the 'jewellery' stolen was worth over 400 *scudi* (almost £8,500); the Governor ordered its return on pain of imprisonment. Pietro reluctantly handed it back, and was forced to raise a loan from Girolamo at an exorbitant rate of interest. In March 1694, he and Violante set out for Rome, leaving Pompilia in a comfortless house with a demanding and increasingly irritable husband and his equally irascible brother and mother.

# TWO

# A Thousand Thousand Kisses

*Everyone says that husbands love their wives,*
*Guard them and guide them, give them happiness;*
*'Tis duty, law, pleasure, religion: well,*
*You see how much of this comes true in mine!*

The tension in the old, cold house in Arezzo noticeably slackened after Pietro and Violante had departed for Rome. While no one in the Franceschini family now thought of Guido's marriage as advantageous, no one could seriously accuse his young wife of being less than dutiful, and she settled into a placid, if not particularly agreeable, life with her husband. Beatrice and Girolamo refrained from criticising the marriage, and Guido looked forward to the child she surely must soon bear him.

However, trouble was brewing in Rome. Pope Innocent XII had announced a year of jubilee during which prayers would be said for peace among all Christian people. During that period pardon would be granted to all those who confessed their sins and attended one of the Roman churches for thirty consecutive days. Violante saw her opportunity not merely to relieve her conscience of a past misdemeanour, but to revenge herself on the overbearing Franceschini family. Soon after she and Pietro returned home, she went to church, confessed, and was instructed to admit to her husband that Pompilia was not in fact her daughter, but the bastard child of some anonymous strumpet.

Pietro at first could not believe it. But Violante was able to give the details of the whole deception. Unable to conceive and fearing that if Pietro died suddenly she would be left entirely without means, she had decided that she must somehow acquire a child and convince everyone that it was hers. So in November 1679 she had sent for a midwife, Angela Biondi, and asked her to find her a baby – perhaps from some woman who had unfortunately found herself pregnant and wanted to dispose of the child. Happily, Signora Biondi already knew of a possible candidate: a destitute widow called Corona Paperozzi had just arrived in Rome from the remote village of Canapina, and was living with her sister, Caterina Fiori. Signora Paperozzi was expecting a child in July, and was prepared to hand it over to someone else, especially if that someone was relatively wealthy and could give the infant a good home.

Violante had immediately made herself a cushion which she wore under her gowns and re-padded from week to week to counterfeit pregnancy. On 16 July the midwife came to Violante at about eleven in the evening to tell her, behind the door, that the child had been born a few hours previously and was already at her house – though she had had some difficulty in persuading the mother to part with it. The following afternoon, Pietro would remember, she had sent him out of the house. Immediately he left, she sent for the midwife, who had come with the baby and her husband, another Pietro, carrying the afterbirth and a flask of calf's blood to which he had added salt, so that it would not clot.

Violante arranged her bed and smeared the bedclothes with the blood ('it wasn't fresh, and was beginning to smell a little', she remembered). Then she got into bed and when the midwife was ready with the rest of the stage effects she began to shriek, for the sake of the neighbours. The midwife placed the baby between her legs, wrapped in an old towel, and pulled the skirts of Violante's taffeta gown over it. Then she called down to the tailor's wife, Signora Boba; when the latter had come and been ordered to support Violante's shoulders, it was the work of but a moment to produce the child as Violante gave one last triumphant cry. (Signora Boba, questioned later, confirmed the story: 'I couldn't see in any way when the child was born – as I was on my knees behind her and she was taller than I, it was impossible . . . and the child was born as all other children were born, except

that it seemed to me that on one arm and on the back
and hair, the blood was rather dry.')

Violante gave the midwife an ell of crimson damask as
a present, and after she had sent her packing asked
Signora Boba to call across the street to Barbara
Caporossi, a friend who lived opposite, and give her the
news. Barbara came over, bringing a chicken as a
present, which was set roasting while Signora Boba
swaddled the child in fresh white linen. Violante's part-
time servant, Petronilla, was sent for while her husband
went to find Pietro and bring him home. The story was
all perfectly circumstantial, so Pietro had to believe it.
Later, in his will, he was to record the fact that both he
and Pompilia herself had been entirely ignorant of her
real parentage, that 'both she and I were tricked . . .
thanks to the vanity of the schemes unfortunately
conceived by my said wife to make me believe in the
birth of my daughter'. Violante had eventually told him
the truth 'because of a scruple of conscience'.

'When I told Signor Pietro about it on my knees',
Violante later said, 'he remained motionless for a
while, and then said these exact words: "However
could you do me this great wrong, and not tell me
about it before? If you had confessed it sooner I should
not have ruined myself and you in this fashion." And he
asked me whether there were others who knew about
this, and I told him yes; and then raising me to my feet
he said to me, "I forgive you." Nor did he say anything

else then. It is true, however, that he did not speak to me for several days.'

When the truth had sunk in, Pietro could scarcely believe that he had ever credited the original story. After all, Violante had been forty-seven when she apparently conceived Pompilia – and they had been trying for a child since their marriage, fourteen years previously. He could do nothing but accept the situation, and indeed he was soon persuaded of his wife's view that the truth provided an excellent weapon with which to revenge themselves on the Franceschini. During May and June he sought out witnesses to support her story, and when he had found them, issued a judicial notice denying paternity and repudiating the dower contract, producing six depositions from, among others, the tailor's wife and an aunt of Pompilia's (her mother and the midwife were both by now dead). In return Guido brought suit on 20 August 1695 for the implementation of the contract. The case was heard by the Auditor Curiae, Joannes Domenicus Thomatus, before whom the six witnesses were produced and swore to Pompilia's illegitimacy.

The evidence of Pietro's witnesses must have been embarrassing for him, for they made it quite clear that even if he had not been aware of Pompilia's true parenthood, a large number of other people had. A certain Agnese Santa Olivieri, for instance, a friend of the midwife Angela – and, it will be remembered, one of Pompilia's wet-nurses – had actually met Angela and her husband as they were carrying the newly born infant to the Comparini's house; she had always known that they were not the true parents. It was unlikely that she would have kept the news entirely to herself, and no doubt there was a considerable amount of sniggering behind Pietro's back.

Pompilia herself, if she ever read the depositions, must have learned the reason for some puzzling incidents in her childhood. She must have remembered, for instance, the occasion when she was at school and a strange, middle-aged woman had suddenly come up to her, caught her in her arms and kissed her. Now she learned that the woman had been her real mother, brought to the school by another daughter – the sister Pompilia did not know she had. The sister was Cristina Paperozzi, who was considerably older than Pompilia, had been brought to Rome by her mother and lived with her at an aunt's house in the Vacuole de'Sediari. Cristina remembered hearing her mother tell her aunt that when she had her baby, she wanted it placed in the hospital of San Spirito, a home for over 500 unwanted infants who were given a religious education and later sent out into the world either as wives or nuns. Cristina remembered her aunt saying that she had a better plan than that: she knew of a rich woman who would take care of the child.

Cristina had been in the house when Pompilia was born, and remembered being slightly bewildered when the afterbirth, usually destroyed, was carefully saved in a basin and taken away with the infant. Later, she remembered her aunt promising to take her mother to show her the house where the child now lived, and four or five years later she, Cristina, had been sent to a school run by a woman called Margherita, four or five doors from the Comparini's house, and had seen there a tiny, well-dressed child aged perhaps four or five, whom they called Checca. 'I told Corona, my mother', the witness said, 'that at the school where I went there was in attendance the daughter of the said Signora Violante called Checca. And when my mother heard this she said that she wanted to come and see her at the said school, and indeed she did go there, and saw and caressed and kissed her . . .'

After hearing the case, Thomatus gave his verdict: for Guido. Why, after all, should he be expected to return a dowry freely offered to him with a wife he understood to be legitimate? But the effect was to recognise Pompilia as the Comparini's child, which seemed ludicrous to Pietro (and one can sympathise). He appealed; a second decision went against him on 17 September. He then went to the Supreme Court, and the case was set down for examination by an Auditor of the Rota, Josephus Molines. But the wheels of the law moved slowly, and the case was never called.

Pietro, however shocked he was by his wife's revelation, could not bring himself to disinherit Pompilia. He was too close to her to be able suddenly to thrust her aside. Indeed, not long after Violante had revealed his daughter's ignoble birth, he made a new will in which he left all his property to his wife – but in the event of her death to 'Francesca Pompilia, wife of Signor Guido Franceschini of Arezzo. I do so because of her good character and because for a long time, yes, for many years, I looked upon her in good faith as my daughter, and thought that Signora Violante, my wife, and myself were her parents.'

Back in Arezzo, however relieved Guido and the family must have been at the court's decision, her parents' assertion of Pompilia's bastardy did nothing to improve relations with the Franceschini. Beatrice in particular was highly uncomfortable at the thought that all her highborn relatives now knew that even if her son had not married the daughter of a whore (for Corona Paperozzi seems to have been an entirely respectable widow), he had certainly been the object of some kind of obscene practical joke.

Guido may have been slightly more sanguine, despite Pietro's refusal to hand over the rest of Pompilia's dowry. He had, after all, a pretty and healthy young wife who, now her parents were out of the way, would be much more tractable, and would no doubt in time fulfil her main purpose – to provide him with an heir. Or would she? After nine months there was still no sign of this, despite Guido's best efforts. Nor did those efforts show any result over the following two years. Guido consulted all the authorities and obeyed their injunctions: not, for instance, to make love to Pompilia too frequently – for frequent intercourse weakened the semen. There were various opinions on the matter. Lorenzo Gioberti in his *Degli errori populari (On Popular Errors)* of 1591, still regarded in the late seventeenth century as a reliable expert, suggested building up the strength of the semen by refraining from intercourse for at least two or three weeks – though Guido, when the blood was hot, turned rather to Savonarola, who regarded a pause of five days as more appropriate. Then there was the temperature of the bedroom: if it was too cold, a chilled uterus would work against procreation; so Beatrice was persuaded that a good fire in the bedroom was now necessary. Hot baths were prepared, warm douches and flushes. A piece of garlic was placed in Pompilia's vagina, and her breath carefully savoured: if there was no hint of garlic on it, then there was some fatal blockage in the generative organs (the girl learned early to chew a little garlic before the test was made). Her genitals were strewn with a finely chopped concoction of galangal, marjoram and mushrooms to encourage sexual ardour and therefore conception; she was even suspended over a cauldron containing hot wine in which had been mixed nettle, oregano, fennel, cumin, mallow, mint, anise and coriander, so that the vapours could rise and thoroughly infiltrate her body.

Surprisingly, she still failed to conceive. However, she seemed to have been brought round to the Franceschini's view of her parents, for in a letter to her brother-in-law Abate Paolo in Rome, dated 14 June 1694, she wrote:

Dearest Brother-in-law,

I wish by this letter to pay my respects to you, and to thank you for your efforts in placing me in this home, where, far removed from my parents, I live now a tranquil life and enjoy perfect safety, not having them around me. For they grieved me day and night with their perverse commands, which were against the law, both human and divine: that I should not love Signor Guido, my husband, and that I should flee by night from his couch. At the same time they made me tell him that I had no congeniality with him and that he was not my husband because I have no children by him. They also caused me to run away often to the Bishop without any reason whatever, and made me tell the Bishop that I wished to be divorced from Signor Guido. And for the purpose of stirring up great discord in the home, my mother told the Bishop and Signor Guido, and then the entire town, that the Canon my brother-in-law [Girolamo] had solicited me dishonourably, a thing that had never been thought of by him. They urged me to continue these evil counsels, which were far from right and far from the submission due to my husband. And they left me at their departure their express command, by my obligation to obey them, that I should kill my husband, give poison to my brothers-in-law and my mother-in-law, burn the house and break the vases and other things, in order that in the eyes of the world it might not appear after their departure that it was they who had counselled me to commit so many crimes. And finally at their departure, they left me, as a parting command, that I should choose for myself a young man to my taste, and with him should run away to Rome, and many other matters, which I omit for blushing.

Now that I have not her at hand who stirred up my mind, I enjoy the quiet of Paradise, and know that my parents were thus directing me to a precipice, because of their own rage. Therefore, now that I see in their true light these deeds proposed by the command of my parents, I pray for pardon from God, from yourself, and from all the world. For I wish to be a good Christian and a good wife to Signor Guido, who has many times chidden me in a loving manner, saying that some day I would thank him for the reproofs he gave me. And these evil counsels, which my parents have given, I have now made known, and I acknowledge myself.

Your most affectionate servant and sister,

FRANCESCA FRANCHESCHINI *née* COMPARINI

Paolo, who had no doubt heard from Guido and possibly from Girolamo of the Comparini's behaviour, thought the letter rather on the hysterical side. The Comparini were certainly not particularly desirable in-laws – he had never thought they would be – but was he to believe that they had seriously proposed the mass slaughter of the family by the fourteen-year-old bride? He rewarded Pompilia's confidence in his friendship by sending her the present of a fan, but he also wrote to the Vincenzo Marzi-Medici, Governor of Arezzo, and asked what he knew about the situation in town. The Governor replied on 2 August (with the deference due to his fellow townsman's position):

My most Illustrious and Dearly Beloved Master,

Your favoured letter of the twenty-fourth of last month has reached me, and I am exceedingly sorry for the uneasiness in which you hint you are placed by the maledictions which Signor Pietro Comparini and his wife have disseminated throughout Rome concerning the ill-treatment they say they suffered in your home while staying in Arezzo.

As your letter questions me for true information, I answer with all frankness that both among the noble connection and in Count Guido's house [Signor and Signora Comparini] were treated with all respect and decorum. The cause of the first disturbance which sprang up between them and your mother and brothers was that

Signora Violante, a few days after her arrival, presumed to domineer over the house and to keep the keys of everything, and in fact to turn out of house and home Signora Beatrice, your mother. With good reason, neither of the brothers was willing to consent thereto, and this gave occasion for the first insults and domestic broils. These afterwards increased when they saw that Signor Pietro had given over the company and conversation of the best people of the city, and had struck up acquaintances with the most vulgar. And with them he began to frequent daily all the taverns here. This cast discredit upon him, and was little for the good name of the Franceschini.

Of much greater scandal were the many flights and petitions made by Guido's wife, their daughter, to Monsignor the Bishop. These were made for no other reason than that neither she nor her parents wished to stay any longer in Arezzo, but desired to return to Rome. When she had been rebuked by that most prudent Prelate, he always sent her home in his carriage.

It is true that ever since the Comparini left this City until the present time the Signora has conducted herself with much modesty and prudence. From this fact every one infers that the poor child was led to such excesses by her parents, as she herself declares to everybody. Now she detests even the memory of them. Therefore she is getting back into the good opinion of every one, and especially of those ladies of the city who had ceased having anything to do with her.

Finally, these same Comparini had taken away all her jewellery from the Signora, which I forced them to restore.

Altogether, such and so great are the scandals to which they have given rise before the whole city in the lapse of the few months they have stayed here, that I write you only a few of them. I assure you that with them your brothers have had the patience of martyrs. Accordingly, when I saw that they had become incorrigible, and were the talk of the town, and that they might force your brothers to commit some excess against them, for the maintenance of good discipline I availed myself of the authority vested in me by His Serene Highness and threatened them with prison and punishment unless they behaved themselves. After these threats, which they evidently merited and which might have overtaken them, they decided to go to Rome, as they did a little later, leaving behind them in this city a very bad reputation.

As for the rest, there is now in your home an utter quietude, and the Signora lives with exemplary prudence, detesting the ill example she had shown the ladies of this city, and she confesses freely that it was so commanded by her parents.

In my judgement, it is the hand of God that has freed your family from such turbid heads. This is all I can here put down, out of much else there is to say about it. Therefore rest at ease, and believe me that the discredit has been entirely their own. I need only sign myself, with all my heart, to your most illustrious self, your most devoted and obliged servant,

VINCENZO MARZI-MEDICI

The Governor was eager to be of use to the distinguished Secretary of the Order of St John of Malta; he exaggerated the number of appeals Pompilia had made to the Bishop – and very possibly her present apparently placid state of mind. The Abate was lulled into a sense of security that turned out to be overconfident. Pompilia's failure to conceive gradually became a serious thorn in her husband's side, and though at first he blamed her parents – claiming to have heard Pietro confess that some concoction administered to her by a quack doctor for a childhood illness had made her sterile – both he and Beatrice believed the girl herself to be at least unenthusiastic about conceiving. She may, indeed, have been a less than ardent lover.

Not that Pompilia had an entirely unpleasant time of it, and for several months she seems to have been reasonably content with her way of life. The family often took refuge from the heat of summer at their farm on the cool hills at Vitiano, and even in town she was not a prisoner: a middle-aged and by no means handsome husband with a beautiful young wife is unlikely not to want to show her off, and Guido, though careful of her honour and his own, took her out to parties and to the opera, and introduced her to his brother-in-law Canon Conti and a number of the Canon's younger friends. He did not altogether approve of some of them, but after all, Canon Conti was a member of one of the most distinguished families in the city, so . . .

One evening during the sort of horseplay that was usual during the opera (few people came to the theatre actually to listen to Sartorio's *L'Adelaide* or Pallavicino's *Vespasiano*) some sweets – described as 'confetti', today sugared almonds – were thrown into Pompilia's lap. Guido took serious offence at this, and, turning rapidly, thought he saw the culprit – a certain Canon Giuseppe Maria Caponsacchi, sitting next to Conti. In fact, Conti himself had thrown the candy, but Caponsacchi did not trouble himself to deny the accusation, and there was a certain amount of ragging of the quick-tempered and over-solemn Guido. Pompilia was delightedly amused – she needed a little light-hearted diversion. The incident became a private joke between Pompilia and the attractive young Giuseppe, and when he and Conti called on Guido – which Conti seemed to do more often, during the next year, than he had previously done – it was the cause of a certain amount of giggling.

Giuseppe was twenty-two when he was first introduced to Pompilia (he had been born on 26 May 1673). He was a Canon of Santa Maria della Pieve, the largest and most beautiful Romanesque church in the Arezzo region, and when he was twenty had been made sub-deacon. This did not mean that he was a priest, however. Someone described as a canon was often merely the holder of a benefice – the right to revenues from a parish – who paid a cleric to carry out the liturgical duties of a canon, and while we do not know whether Giuseppe was such a canon, there is no evidence at all that he took part in any ecclesiastical duties. A sub-deacon was a low-ranking ecclesiastic, one who presented the chalice and paten at the offertory and removed them after the communion, but did not actually officiate at the Mass. Giuseppe did not hold holy orders and never had the faintest ambition to be a priest. He was merely a good-looking and carelessly flirtatious young gallant with an elegant taste in clothes (his silver-trimmed black hat was much admired by his friends), who strolled about the streets and piazza with a short sword at his side, like an extra in some romantic comedy.

He must have seemed to Pompilia a ready-made romantic hero, and she was ready for one. One of the few pleasures she had been able to cultivate at Arezzo was reading – the Franceschini house contained a small library, and she had access to books which she had lacked at her parents' house. The evidence presented later in court suggests that she enjoyed young

Giuseppe's attentions with all the pleasure of a young girl who had been thrust from childhood into marriage without any opportunity to enjoy the romantic friendships of adolescence. She often saw him from her window, with one girl or another on his arm – 'hussies', she jealously called them. But he almost always glanced up at her as he passed, and the regularity with which he called at the house seemed to her to be significant – surely he did not call for the pleasure of talking with her saturnine husband?

The same idea gradually occurred to Guido, and the glances and smiles exchanged between the young people while his brother-in-law engaged him in conversation – at the family house or in the gardens of the farm at Vitiano – did not escape him. Jealousy took hold, and grew; and before long Giuseppe's calls became so much a cause of scenes (though always after his departure) that Pompilia reluctantly took to making some excuse to leave the room whenever the two friends arrived. Guido's suspicions were actually fuelled by this action. It seemed an even more obvious sign of her interest in the young man. She took care not to go anywhere near the window when her husband was nearby, lest he should think she was watching for Giuseppe. And when she did, for a moment, see the young man alone, she asked him to avoid walking along the street below, in case Guido should think it was by appointment.

Giuseppe was incredulous. He could not believe that Guido should suspect such a thing. He passed by because he had business which brought him that way; it would be extremely inconvenient to take any other route. Surely . . . but as Pompilia was about to explain further, Guido entered the room. Now she could only continue to avoid being anywhere near the window when her husband was nearby. His suspicions continued to grow, however. The incident at the theatre had taken root in his mind, and seemed to be both the beginning of an illicit romance and the symbol of it.

It was true that over the past months a close relationship had grown up between the two young people. Taking care to do so only when Guido was out of the way, Pompilia began to watch for Giuseppe. Her instinct told her that she was of more interest to him than the minxes who still clung to his arm. As for him, he was young and hot-blooded. A ravishing young wife making eyes at him was a temptation not to be resisted. She wrote him a note. He replied, via a compliant maid, Maria. The notes grew longer and warmer. He began lending her books – Marino's sensual poem *Adone*, Morandi's romantic *Rosalinda*, the moral ending of which for some religious readers failed to excuse its erotic passages. They began a regular exchange of letters. Those that have survived and are reprinted in the *Yellow Book* are undated, and it is difficult to guess at their order; but it is clear that affection between the two quickly intensified. He sent her verses of his own, which she described as 'indecent' without forbidding him to send more. Soon she was addressing him as Mirtillo, and signed herself Amarillis – they were characters from Guarini's play *Il pastor fido*, who loved each other, but Amarillis was betrothed to another man. Pompilia apologised for not meeting his eyes when they last met: her husband and his mother had been watching her. 'But after all, your picture is engraved on my heart . . .'

Soon, she was signing herself 'your faithful Sweetheart', and sending him 'a million kisses – though they are not so dear as a few would be if you would give them to me'. She put his letters in her breast, next to her heart, until she was forced to burn them lest Guido should find them. On one occasion he picked one of them up, but she had tied it together with some other, innocent letters, and he put them down without examining them.

Now, she regularly came to her window so that at least she could see Giuseppe, even if it was better that he did not look up at her, for she had reason to believe that Guido or his mother were continually watching the street. Yet if he did not appear, she wrote rebuking him: she had spent ages looking, and there had been no sign of him – she had gone to several of the windows of the house, but he was not to be seen. He was being too cautious – he should not think that her mother-in-law spent every hour watching out for him: when he thought he had seen her acting suspiciously at a window, she had only been telling a servant where to place a sofa in the room beyond – 'so you can pass by without fear'.

Occasionally, the situation eased a little: 'None of them has said anything to me – none of them. But Signor Guido seems rather well disposed toward me than otherwise, and therefore I cannot find out whether they are angry with me.' At other times things were more difficult – or perhaps she heightened the drama of the occasion. When they had both attended the same party, 'I pray you pardon me that I did not look at you . . . because I saw that the two were watching to see if I would look at you. Therefore I suffered much pain at not being able to look at my Sun. But I saw mine own with my heart, in which I have you engraved . . .'

She continually fanned Giuseppe's interest. When he broke the game to ask how she could have fallen so in love with him when they had only met socially, she replied:

Either you think me blind, or unfriendly. You *cannot* say that I do not love you – nor can you say that anyone loves you as much as I do. Look into my eyes, and you will be astonished; when they are bright with tears, you will see that your face is copied there, that your

whiteness is snow compared to the Milky Way, that the
Graces themselves direct your movements, that Venus
measured your limbs with her own girdle! . . . I want
everyone in the world to love you, because then I can
prove that all of them together cannot love you as much
as I. My heart is envied by every other part of me,
because it is the only part of me that is able to love you
. . . I leave you a thousand thousand kisses.

None of Giuseppe's surviving letters is as overtly
passionate as that, but clearly there was warmth on his
side. The affair ripened: Conti, who carried many of
the letters to and fro, soon had to warn Giuseppe of
Guido's increasing jealousy – and the young man wrote
to Pompilia telling her what she already knew: that 'the
Jealous One' had threatened to kill them both if
he discovered them together. Did the affair go further
than an exchange of letters? Was she able to love him
with more than her heart? A certain Maria Margherita
Contenti, who lived opposite the Franceschini house
and may have been a prostitute (Pompilia certainly had
a low opinion of her), reported that on one occasion
when Guido was away from home: 'At the sound of
the Ave Maria, while I was at the window, I saw the
door of the Signori Franceschini open very softly, and
from it passed the said Signor [Caponsacchi] . . . He
pulled the door to as he went out, but did not in fact
close it, and therefrom, after a little while I saw

Signora Francesca Pompilia with a light in her hand close the door.'

On one occasion Pompilia was careful to tell Giuseppe that 'I stay in the same room as at first . . . I have told the servant that she should make the signals agreed upon, etc. Signor Guido returns Saturday morning, and you may pass this evening at ten o'clock or sooner, when you shall see the light in the room, etc.' In another letter she told Giuseppe not to come to her, though Guido was away, 'because the street door is no longer open, though you might be able to open the back door . . .' And, in another, 'Signor Guido is going out of the city, and will be gone several days. Therefore I pray you come this evening about seven o'clock, and when you are under the window cough and wait a little while, that I may not make a mistake.' Another flirtatious letter later came to light, which seemed to have been thrown down from her window, in which she asked him to 'come here this evening at the same hour as the day before yesterday [in the] evening . . . But if you do not wish to come here (so that you avoid breaking your promise to some beloved lady) I do not wish to be the cause. So if you wish to come here, walk on as soon as you have read this.'

Did Pompilia decide to flee, in the end, because she discovered that she was pregnant, and not by her husband? Whether or not Pompilia and Giuseppe came closer together than an exchange of eyes from street to window, they certainly reached an understanding. Life at Arezzo had become insupportable to her. She was regarded as a useless wife. Continually reminded that her husband's line was to be brought to an end because she could not bear him a child, she was now accused, every day, of being unfaithful to him. Not that the idea was repugnant to her, even if her experience of sex was not so pleasant as to send her after a lover. She was still in her mid-teens, a child as far as that was concerned, inexperienced except in the embraces of a husband whose love-making was constrained by the often eccentric instructions of 'experts' on the best way to conceive. Desperate, she began to think of her parents in Rome. Even if it was true that they were not really blood relatives, they had never been unkind to her – if she excepted their marrying her to Guido, and they could never have foreseen how unkind he might become. Moreover, a recent letter had spoken of Pietro's being seriously ill. Surely it was her duty to consider this, and at least to visit them? But there would be no point in making such a suggestion to her husband.

Who could help her? Who *would* help her? She wrote to her parents in Rome, but received no answer. She went yet again to Bishop Marchetti; she was heard, but only heard – he offered no advice except that she should remain with her husband and be obedient to his wishes. He then sent her home in his carriage once again. She had met a kindly priest, a Fra Romano, at the Pieve, and made her confession to him. Like his Bishop, he merely impressed upon her the necessity of obedience to her lord and master. She asked Conti for his help, and he must surely have felt obliged to take her appeal seriously. After all, it had been he who had brought her and Giuseppe together in a flirtation that had seriously offended his brother-in-law and caused him to behave offensively to Pompilia. There is little evidence of Conti's attitude to Guido, but he seems to have had no great respect for him, while he may have regarded Giuseppe as a surrogate son (he himself had no children).

At all events he seems to have decided that the best thing would be for Pompilia to leave Arezzo at least for a time – a cooling-off period after which perhaps some new accommodation could be reached. He suggested that an acquaintance of his, Gregorio Guillichini, a young nobleman also distantly related to the Franceschini family who knew, admired and felt sorry for Pompilia (he had once been seen throwing snowballs up at her window in an innocently flirtatious sort of way), might be prepared to escort her to Rome and her parents' home. Indeed, Guillichini went so far as to send a message to them asking for reassurance that they would accept her if she came home to them. They immediately replied in the affirmative, but then Guillichini either fell ill or made the excuse that he was ill, and vanished from the scene.

The only person left who might be persuaded to help her was Giuseppe, and by degrees she persuaded him to do so. The hints of their plan come obliquely through in the letters, when Pompilia begins to reply to her lover's questions about the drinking habits of her husband and his family. Sometimes her mother-in-law felt unwell and drank nothing. At other times she and Guido drank red wine, 'but I do not know how much longer it will be so'. Again, 'If they continue to drink red wine, I will tell you so.' The point was, of course, that a drug is less likely to be discerned in red wine than in white.

The moment came when a move had to be made, and promptly. 'On Wednesday,' Giuseppe wrote her,

the Bishop departs with three carriages. If you cannot leave tomorrow evening, God knows when you shall be able to do so, because of the scarcity of carriages. If you can go, as soon as you read this letter, throw it back to me from the window as a sign that I may reserve a carriage beforehand. If I secure the carriage tomorrow, in passing by I will let my handkerchief fall. For the rest, tomorrow evening I will wait from eight o'clock in the evening or as long as necessary. As soon as you see that they are sound asleep, open the door to me, that I may help you make up your bundles and collect the money. Above all, try to put some [opium] into all their cups, and do not yourself drink it. And if by ill luck they shall find it out, and shall threaten you with death, open indeed the door, that I may die with you or free you from their hands.

So it had come to this. Giuseppe was so much in love that he would prefer to die with her than to escape without her.

On the evening of Sunday 28 April 1697, Pompilia successfully slipped a draft of opium into the wine drunk by her husband and his mother. She got into bed with Guido, and waited until he was soundly asleep. Then she got up, dressed, and began to collect a few things together. The more of her possessions she picked up, the more she wanted to take. Giuseppe, who now joined her, must have been rather embarrassed as he watched the collection grow.

First, with the key taken from her husband's discarded trousers, Pompilia opened his strong-box, and took a bag containing some gold coins (about 200 *scudi* or some £4,240, Guido later alleged), then an oriental pearl necklace, a pair of diamond pendants, a solitaire diamond ring, a gold ring with a turquoise setting, an amber necklace, a pair of earrings in the shape of tiny golden ships set with tiny pearls, a coronet of carnelians and other miscellaneous jewellery, and finally a silver snuff-box bearing the Franceschini family arms. Giuseppe turned, ready to leave. But Pompilia understandably wanted to take some clothing, too. She went to the wardrobes. A damask suit, a petticoat embroidered with poppies, another light-blue petticoat decorated with white flowers, two vests, two pairs of point lace sleeves, a lace collar, a black taffeta scarf, two lace aprons, a pair of scarlet silk boots, a pair of wool stockings – it seemed that she was now no longer choosing, but gathering up everything she saw . . . a snuff-coloured worsted bodice and a petticoat embroidered with red and white pawns, a petticoat of striped light-blue and orange, four linen smocks, a pair of shoes with silver buckles, two pairs of gloves, four handkerchiefs. When she picked up four table napkins, Giuseppe lost patience, took her arm and hurried her away. The goods they took with them were worth more than 400 *scudi* – almost £8,500 – according to the list that Guido later compiled.

Outside the house Gregorio Guillichini, who had recovered sufficiently to see the couple on their way, was waiting. At the Horse Inn outside the San Clemente gate stood a *calese*, with the two horses Giuseppe had ordered from the Canale Inn, opposite the Pieve church. The gate, like the others of the city, was closed, as they expected. They had to find a way of climbing the city walls. Guillichini carried the unexpectedly large burden of Pompilia's clothing and the jewellery up the hill of the Torrione, where once a solid defensive tower stood. There, the city wall was low on the inside and easy to climb. They mounted it, dropped to the ground, then walked around the outside of the walls until they came to the waiting *calese*. It was one o'clock in the morning.

Guillichini stacked the bundle as best he might, and the fleeing couple climbed into the vehicle behind the driver, Francesco Giovanni de'Rossi, known as Venerino, a servant from the Canale Inn. Far from being a comfortable carriage, it was merely a two-wheeled cart through whose unsprung body every stone and rut in the road towards Perugia and on to Rome sent a rude shock. The route they chose was along the Consular road, by way of Foligno and the Via Flaminia – not the shortest way, but because of the state of the road, the quickest. Whipped on by their eagerness Venerino made remarkable time, considering the darkness of the night (the Moon set as they were leaving the town). When Goethe went the same way in 1786, he took six days to travel from Perugia to Rome, and thought he had done well.

It was a highly uncomfortable journey in the kindest of circumstances. Even a hundred years later a travel writer was advising extreme care when using the Consular road because of highwaymen and footpads, wolves and bears, and pointing out that the roughness of the road was very like to induce sickness and vomiting even in the most practised of travellers. Even so, it was a great deal better than the alternative: a cross-country route that was almost impassable except by single horses – most wheels would shatter on the track, which was almost indistinguishable from the rough ground around it.

Two horses could not take them all the way to Rome; post-houses supplied replacements at suitable but irregular intervals – sometimes as little as six miles, sometimes as many as seventeen. Between Arezzo and Rome there were at least twenty of these changes, and before they were forced to rest the fleeing couple passed through fourteen. This cost them over £100 in today's currency, quite apart from their fretting at the necessary delays. Guido later claimed that they paused long enough at Foligno to sleep together there, but could produce no proof to confirm the allegation – and it seems extremely unlikely that the most passionate of lovers would pause for love-making when they knew that an irate husband might be close behind them. At least they could take a quick bite of bread and a cup of wine to sustain them before they pressed on. When day broke, and there was no sign of pursuit, they were able to take the journey a little more easily, and after over forty hours on the road they reached the little village of Castelnuovo, about fifteen miles from Rome. Though it would only have taken them another few hours to reach the city, both the fleeing couple and the driver were exhausted. Giuseppe took a room for the night. A servant gave evidence, at the trials, that it was a single room.

Guido awoke from his muddied sleep, and though drowsy from the effects of the drug he had been given, he soon discovered the absence both of Pompilia and of the contents of the strong box, the lid of which stood open, the key still in the lock. He knew immediately what had happened. Why had he not accepted the advice of his sister Porzia, who had overheard scraps of suspicious conversation between Giuseppe and her husband, Conti, and warned him that some plot was brewing?

He guessed that his wife must be making for Rome, and the inference was that Giuseppe was with her and had helped her plan her escape – where would a child have been able to come by the narcotic which was still somewhat fuddling his mind? In a small city where most people knew each other, he did not have to make many enquiries before confirming that Giuseppe Caponsacchi had also left Arezzo during the night. He took to horse, and rode off in the direction of Rome. At the post-houses – Torricella, Madonna degli Angeli, Spoleto, Terni, Borghetto and the rest – it was easy to confirm that a *calese* bearing a young couple had preceded him. He was only five or six hours, at most, behind them, and a single man on horseback has the advantage over three people in a carriage.

Early in the morning of 1 May he approached Castelnuovo. Just outside the town, a dusty and bedraggled *calese* stood outside an inn, and at its side under the roughly arched stone portico was Giuseppe, who had just ordered up the horses to continue the journey to Rome. Guido confronted him, sword in hand. He took one step towards the younger man, who drew his own sword, confronting Guido with the words: 'I am a man, and have done what I have that I might save your wife from death.' This only infuriated Guido more – but he hesitated; in Arezzo, the rumour had been that Caponsacchi was carrying fire-arms. Moreover, at that moment Pompilia – so some onlookers later swore – came from the inn, seized the sword from Giuseppe, and ran at her husband. Guido backed down, only to go to the Governor's house and make a complaint against the two fugitives, who were arrested and taken to the solid and forbidding Pretura, accused under the *Processus Fugae*, or Prosecution for Elopement.

# THREE

# A Prosecution for Elopement

*. . . a worm must turn*
*If it would have its wrong observed by God.*

AProsecution for Elopement was not unusual. Roman men guarded their wives' virtue with the greatest vigour. Men who did not go nearly so far as eloping with a woman had for years been prosecuted for taking a lesser liberty: since the time of the anti-pope Benedict XIV (1425–30) the Roman Criminal Code had included a firm rule against 'kissing a woman of good character in public'. 'Whoever shall violently assault, and kiss, or try to kiss, a virtuous woman, in public – even though he should not actually succeed in kissing her, but should only proceed so far as an embrace, – shall be condemned to the galleys for life; shall have his possessions confiscated; and shall even be liable to the penalty of death.' By the end of the seventeenth century that law, though still on the books, was very rarely exercised – but eloping with, and making love to, a married woman was naturally much more culpable, and the guilty party could scarcely expect a lesser sentence than death. Moreover, that sentence could be imposed instantly on a wife and her lover by a husband who caught them in the act of adultery. Though he would certainly be brought before the courts, he would equally certainly not suffer the death penalty.

In the case of Pompilia and Giuseppe, evidence was needed that she had indeed eloped with Giuseppe in the legal sense of the word, rather than that he had merely assisted her to escape from cruel captivity in her husband's house (although even that would not be regarded as a light matter).

After having Pompilia and Giuseppe arrested at Castelnuovo, Guido instigated a careful search of the room they had occupied. The searchers found nothing – but minutes later he was shown a bedraggled clutch of papers which had been found in the nearby latrine. They appeared to be love-letters between Pompilia and her lover. Importantly, it was later claimed on Guido's behalf that the letters were found as the result of a search ordered not by him, but by the Vicar-General. If this was the case, it is clearly much less likely that (as both Giuseppe's and Pompilia's lawyers suggested) Guido had forged the letters and hidden them in the latrine. If further argument on this point took place either in the elopement trial or the later one, it has not survived.

From the prison at Arezzo, Pompilia wrote a confused note to Pietro and Violante:

My dear father and mother,

I wish to inform you that I am imprisoned here in Castelnuovo for having fled from home with a gentleman with whom you are not acquainted. But he is a relative of the Guillichini, who was at Rome, and who was to have accompanied me to Rome. As Guillichini was sick and could not come with me, the other gentleman came, and I came with him for this reason, because my life was not worth an hour's purchase. For Guido my husband wished to kill me, because he had certain suspicions, which were not true, and on account of these he wished to murder me. I sent you word of them on purpose, but you did not believe the letters sent you were in my own hand. But I declare that I finished learning how to write in Arezzo. Let me tell you that the one who carries this was moved by pity and provided me with the paper and what I needed. So soon as you have read this letter of mine come here to Castelnuovo to give me some aid, because my husband is doing all he can against me. Therefore if you wish your daughter well, come quickly. I stop because I have no more time. May 3.

An interesting point in this letter, which none of the lawyers appears to have made, is that it seems to show that Pompilia did not in the first place plan to abscond with Giuseppe, but that she asked if she could accompany Guillichini to Rome, that he agreed that she could do so, and that she told her parents this. If he had not fallen ill, it may well be that they would have travelled together to

Rome, that Guido would not have been likely to accuse them of adultery, and that the case against his wife and Giuseppe would have been much weaker. The phrase 'finished learning to write' is also significant.

The accused couple were now carried the fifteen miles to Rome and taken to the Carceri Nuove, the New Prisons, in the Via Giulia, very near the Palazzo Farnese – a forbidding building put up some forty years earlier, replacing the ancient prisons of the Torre di Nono, which had stood near the Ponte Sant'Angelo. The Carceri Nuove were not 'new' in any sense that the building was any less forbidding or uncomfortable than the earlier one. Sir Frederick Treves, in Rome in 1900, found it still much as the eloping couple, and later Guido, would have remembered it:

> The long stone corridors are vaulted and unusually lofty. The end of each corridor is closed by a merciless iron gate and grille. With few exceptions the prisoners were herded together in large, airy cells, capable of taking from twelve to fourteen beds. These cells have a cove roof or a vaulted ceiling, in each angle of which is a large star. This curious and inspiring ornament is the only one the designer of the jail allowed himself to use. The windows are blocked with heavy bars, while the opening through the outer wall of the jail being on different levels, it is impossible for a prisoner to see anything from his room but a patch of sky . . .

Pompilia and Giuseppe were closely followed to Rome by Guido, whose friends found him almost delirious with rage at the affronts to his honour. They tried to comfort him: at least Pompilia's flight now made clear her unfitness to be his wife, the marriage could be easily dissolved, and he could retain the dowry. He was not much cheered, and could not bear the thought of attending his wife's trial. On 7 October he persuaded and authorised his brother Paolo to look after all his affairs in Rome, especially 'the carrying on and defending . . . all lawsuits and causes, civil or mixed, already brought or to be brought for any reason whatsoever, and against any persons whatsoever, anywhere, and especially in Rome, whether as plaintiff or defendant before any judge . . .' He then went back to Arezzo, where he immediately laid a complaint before the episcopal court, producing for the first time (through his own lawyer, Giovanni Maria Serbuceri) the account of his marriage and Pompilia's perfidy which was to be repeated at the forthcoming trial for elopement, and later at the second trial. Meanwhile, Abate Paolo Franceschini went to the ecclesiastical authorities in Rome for advice on the validity of the marriage, should Pompilia be found guilty.

The Comparini were not particularly concerned about the coming case. Pietro positively boasted to his friends of Pompilia's high spirits and the wit with which she had managed to escape her husband, taking with her a considerable portion of the property to which she was entitled. The Franceschini had better look to themselves. No court was likely to give judgement against such an oppressed wife; he and Violante knew all too well the conditions under which she had been forced to live at Arezzo. Before long she would be back at home with them, and the dowry would be returned. So Pietro, on behalf of his daughter, began proceedings for divorce.

Robert Browning knew almost nothing about the conduct of the Prosecution for Elopement, simply because no documents in his *Yellow Book* described it. However, two documents in the Cortona Codex report first Serbuceri's argument on Guido's behalf, and then Antonio Lamparelli's reply in defence of Giuseppe Caponsacchi, when the trial of the latter for abduction and theft opened in September 1697 in the court of the Governor of Rome under the Deputy Governor, Marco Antonio Venturini. Pompilia and the driver Rossi, together with the unfortunate Gregorio Guillichini, were later tried in the same court. No documentation has been found of their prosecution or defence, though references show that evidence was given for and against them. Fortunately, it was repeated in the later trial for murder, and we can safely assume that it did not change in the meantime.

In Italian law of the period, the state undertook the defence as well as the prosecution of an accused person, and defence lawyers were just as likely to be distinguished and respected men as those who appeared for the prosecution. However determined a lawyer may be not to become emotionally involved in a case, he sometimes falls in love with a defendant – perhaps to some extent he must – and Lamparelli fell so completely under the spell of Pompilia's beauty that until the end of his life he believed in her innocence.

The cases against Caponsacchi, Pompilia and the others may at first glance have seemed simple; in fact, they dragged on for four months. As to the event itself there could be no question: Pompilia had fled from her husband's house and Giuseppe had helped her. There had certainly been an elopement. But had there been adultery? Had Giuseppe really abducted Guido's wife 'because of lust'? Had she truly 'given herself up to dishonest amours' with Giuseppe? Serbuceri, for the Fisc, began his submission to the elopement trial by baldly stating what he claimed to be the facts: that the lovers had planned to dope Guido before breaking the locks of a trunk and stealing cash and jewellery, and that in this matter Giuseppe was as guilty as Pompilia. Guido had compiled a long list of the goods and money his wife and her lover had taken from his house at Arezzo and 'converted to their own uses'. If there was any doubt of the true facts of the case, the court need only remember the events at Castelnuovo, where a number of letters exchanged between the lovers had been found in a latrine at the inn. These letters would be produced to the court, and there could be no doubt of their provenance: together with them a licence had been found referring to Caponsacchi's possible entrance into a monastery, and though Pompilia might claim that she could not write, the evidence was otherwise – her signature appeared on the marriage contracts. A hand-writing expert should be engaged to examine them, to establish the fact. This is the only reference in the documents we have to what seems a very obvious appeal. Why no handwriting expert was invited to examine the letters and compare the signature on them with that on the marriage contracts, is a mystery. Perhaps at the later trial, when evidence was given that Pompilia had attended school and learned to write, such an examination was considered unnecessary.

Serbuceri devoted some time – as Roman lawyers always did – to producing a great number of authorities to show that the circumstances of the abduction made it a 'real' one; it was suggested that for this to be the case, violence must have been exercised towards the woman. None had taken place in this case – but, the lawyer argued, violence had certainly been offered to the husband, which to all effects was the same thing. There was plenty of proof in Pompilia's letters to her lover that the pair had planned to drug Guido. The defence would argue that Pompilia had been abducted to save her from death. This was a 'frivolous and ridiculous' excuse, and there was absolutely no evidence to support it. Moreover, Pompilia contradicted herself: first she said that Guido wanted to kill her because of her sterility, then that he wanted to kill her because he was jealous of her friendship with Giuseppe. At the same time Giuseppe argued that Guido planned to kill Pompilia because of his disagreement with her father. The letters which the court could examine did not contain a single reference to the wife's being threatened by the husband, to her experiencing undue poverty or ill-treatment, or to any physical attacks. The tangle of arguments reduced the defence to nothing. It was surely crystal clear, since the letters were full of expressions of affection, references to jealousy, hints of exchanged kisses, that lust had been the true motive for the abduction.

Did adultery actually took place? Could the court doubt it? Serbuceri quoted Ovid's *Art of Love* – no maiden could return a virgin from the presence of a young and passionate lover. There was evidence that Giuseppe used to visit the Franceschini house at night, and that their relationship was notorious in Arezzan gossip. Then, consider the fact that at Castelnuovo when they were shown into a single room in which there were two beds, Caponsacchi had ordered only one to be prepared! That might be accepted as innocent had Giuseppe been an old man, or if it had been the dead of bitterly cold winter. But he was a young and virile man, and she an attractive young woman. Serbuceri rested his case.

Replying for the defence of a young man he described as of 'upright character and inborn nobility', Lamparelli admitted that a wife's flight from her husband in the company of a man of Giuseppe's age might seem suspicious to the ill-informed, but that when the court looked at all the circumstances it was surely quite clear that the so-called abduction was necessary in order to return to her parents a young woman who was far from her home, ill-treated by husband and in-laws, reduced to such desperation that she appealed to the Bishop and the Governor of Arezzo, and when they failed her, and only then, to the accused. (The lawyer seems not to have made the point that Pompilia had appealed first to Guillichini, although surely Pompilia would have told him about it.)

It was a horrifying thought (Lamparelli went on) that a man was prepared to drag his wife before the court and accuse her of being an adulteress, simply in order to assure himself of possession of her dowry. But that is what the court must believe. He then went through the whole story from the point of view of the absconding lovers, underlining Pompilia's unhappiness, rehearsing again the bitter arguments between Guido and Paolo on one side and the Comparini on the other. He cited many legal authorities at every turn of the plot to support his argument that the flight had been necessary and justified in order to save Pompilia not only from unhappiness but from an early grave – something Giuseppe had put to Guido himself when they confronted each other at Castelnuovo: 'I am an honourable man,' Caponsacchi had said, 'and I did what I have done to remove your wife from the danger of death.' As for Serbuceri and his quotations from Ovid – bah! There were innumerable examples in literature which showed that a young woman could be honourably treated by the most virile young man.

Giuseppe gave his name before the court, and confirmed that he was a Canon of the Pieve, but merely a sub-deacon, and that he had no occupation. He had been planning a visit to Rome just at about the time when Pompilia first approached him – she might have heard of the proposed journey from Conti, to whom he had certainly mentioned it, though in fact it was common knowledge. He had been surprised to receive a letter from the Countess Franceschini – delivered by a woman servant, Maria – in which Pompilia said she had heard he was going to Rome, and asked him to escort her there because her husband meant to kill her, and she wanted to go to her father for protection.

I sent a reply back by the servant saying that I really didn't want to do anything of that sort; but whenever I passed her house, she threw down notes to me repeating her request. I continued to make the same reply. But one day a working-woman in the house opposite saw her throw me a note, managed to get hold of it, and took it to Count Franceschini. The servant Maria came to me and told me there had been a great commotion, and that Count Franceschini had threatened to kill both his wife and me. I decided that the only way out of a difficult and dangerous situation would be for me to escort the Countess to Rome. So one evening – I can't recall the date – as I was passing the house I showed her a note, and she let down a piece of string and pulled it up. In it, I said that I had decided to help her.

It was on the Sunday evening, the last day of last month – April – that I passed her house and seeing her at a window told her that I had arranged for a carriage for the following morning, and I would wait for her at the San Clemente Gate. She came there alone at about one a.m., we got into the carriage and turned along the wall to go towards San Spirito, in the direction of Perugia. I had arranged the carriage with Agostino, the tavern-keeper at Arezzo, and the driver was Venerino, one of Agostino's servants.

We drove without stopping anywhere to spend the night, pausing only when we needed to take some food or drink or to change horses, until we reached Castelnuovo on Tuesday evening. Pompilia said that she was in pain, and she didn't have the strength to go on without resting, so she threw herself on a bed in one of the rooms there, and I lay on another bed in the same room. We were both fully clothed. I told the host to call us in three or four hours – but he failed to do so, and the next thing we knew was that the Count had arrived, and had us both arrested.

Giuseppe swore that he had never written any letters to Pompilia except those he had mentioned. The letters he had received from her had been burned before he left Arezzo. Asked whether the letters had been written by herself, he replied: 'I don't know. I suppose she might have written them – but I don't know whether she knows how to write.'

He confirmed that some money and goods had been found in the room at Castelnuovo, and a proper list had been made by the authorities. Pompilia had carried a bundle of clothing and a small box in which she said there were some trinkets, but he did not see them. She had also had a few coins wrapped in a handkerchief. As far as he knew, neither Guido nor the police had found any letters at Castelnuovo, despite a very thorough search.

There were more questions about the arrangements at the inn:

As I said, there were two beds in the room we shared. Only one of these was made up by a maid, for the Countess. She did not undress. I did not order the other bed to be made up, because I did not want to undress.

He was shown a letter addressed to Pompilia which began '*Adorata mia Signora . . .*' and said that it was not in his handwriting, although there was a superficial likeness. The same was true of a second letter alleged to have been written by him. As to the letters supposed to have been written by Pompilia to him:

> I have never received any letters from the Countess concerning anything other than her flight to Rome. I am astonished that it is alleged that she sent me love-letters. The Countess is a modest young woman, and anything like that would have been out of keeping both with her station and her birth. The accusation is false and baseless. I repeat – nothing of the sort was found either at the inn at Castelnuovo, or in the prison there, and if anyone tells me that love-letters were found addressed to me by the Countess, I can only say that that is absolutely untrue.

The whole tone of Caponsacchi's evidence sounds wrong. One does not have to accept Pompilia's version of events, but her lover's account simply does not convince. Without more evidence, we can only assume that the two young people were simply wriggling hard to get out of a net. They wriggled to some effect, and were assisted by a number of people who took their side for a variety of reasons, one of which may certainly have been a general dislike of the Franceschini family.

Turning to the question of the letters, Lamparelli was in very obvious difficulty, and made a number of assertions so wild that it is surprising the court entertained them for a moment (perhaps it did not). First, he said, the letters were not addressed to Giuseppe; then, they were not signed by Pompilia; and in any event they were not really at all passionate or immodest, and moreover were forgeries which could easily have been written and planted in the latrine by Guido. Lamparelli then dealt with evidence which was repeated at the later trial and attempted to diminish the court's confidence in the witnesses by discrediting them, before making two final points: first, that even if it was the case that Guido had spent the night at Castelnuovo in the same bedroom as Pompilia, this was absolutely necessary in order that he might protect her; and second, that in view of Giuseppe's nobility of character the accusation that his client was guilty of theft (in assisting Pompilia to remove the jewellery and clothing from Guido's room) simply could not be entertained. He then rather spoiled this flourish by suggesting that as the crimes of abduction and theft were committed outside the state, Giuseppe could only be punished with a sentence of exile. The court, for whatever reason, accepted his suggestion. Though Giuseppe was found guilty of 'complicity in flight and running away of Francesca Comparini, and for carnal knowledge of the same', he was indeed merely banished for three years to the coastal town of Civita Vecchia.

And here, Caponsacchi vanishes from our story. Even when Pompilia gave birth to what presumably was his child, he made no attempt to visit them – and there was nothing to prevent him asking permission to do so, even if he did not wish to break the conditions of his sentence; nor does he seem to have made any gesture of sympathy after the dreadful events that were to come. One's instinct from the first – that he was a good-looking young man out for a pleasant affair without responsibilities – seems to be the right one. It is unlikely that he was a thief: the money found on him when he was arrested was shown to have been his own; but he is, after all, something less than a hero.

Incidentally, the court does not seem to have enquired as to the whereabouts of the clothes and jewellery; what money was found in Pompilia's possession was returned to the Count, but about the petticoats and bodices, the handkerchiefs and shoes and damask suits and woollen stockings, nothing was said. It may be that the prosecution thought that it would be too simple for the defence to show that it was perfectly reasonable for a wife to take her clothes with her. However, what actually happened to them remains a mystery.

We can only conjecture the course of Pompilia's trial – but we can do so with confidence; the evidence given was repeated, perhaps by deposition, at the murder trial. Through Lamparelli, she put her case strongly. She spoke of the Franceschini's ill-treatment of her parents, and of Guido's rage that she could not conceive.

> He said that because of me the house of Franceschini would die out, and that he had no hope of an heir because he had overheard my father say that when I was very young I had been ill, and my life had been saved only by a medicine which made me sterile. I said that even if that was true, it wasn't my fault – but the whole family continued to ill-treat me, and even threaten my life.

Then, she said, there was her husband's jealousy. He had stopped her even looking out of the windows, and when she sat on the loggia – even though it was on the roof, high above the street – he said that she was there to make love with someone. Eventually, his suspicions had fixed upon Giuseppe.

> He – Giuseppe – only occasionally paused outside the house, when he happened to pass by, to joke with a group of hussies who gathered there. But my husband fumed because he said he only passed by in order to see me. One evening when we were with a crowd of people at the theatre, Canon Conti, my sister-in-law's husband, threw some confetti [see page 57] at me, and my husband

thought Giuseppe had thrown it, and took offence. When we got home, he pointed a pistol at me, and said 'Christ! – what's stopping me from laying you out here and now? Let Caponsacchi watch it, or I'll kill you.' Whenever Conti and Giuseppe came to the house, he was suspicious – and in the end I used to go to my room whenever he came, to avoid more trouble. But then Guido said that I did *that* on purpose, as some kind of trick. I begged Giuseppe not to come by our house because of the trouble it made, but though he promised not to, he still sometimes did – and though I took care to try never to be near a window, my husband still bullied me.

Then, after her calls on the Bishop had proved unhelpful, she turned to plans for running away. When it was clear that Guillichini could not help her, she had gestured to Giuseppe one day when he was passing the house and her husband was out of the way, and had called to him to come in. They had stood on the stairs while she begged him to help her get to Rome and her parents. At first he had refused, but 'I told him it was the duty of a Christian to free a poor woman from death', and at last he agreed. For a while he did nothing, making the excuse that he could not get hold of a carriage; but at last he made the agreed signal – dropping his handkerchief – and the following night she had waited until Guido was asleep (no, there was no question that she drugged him) and left the house.

I took a few things of my own, a little box of bits and pieces, and some money — I don't know exactly how much — from the strong-box. It was all my own. They have made a list here at Castelnuovo, which will prove it. Then at dawn I went downstairs where I found Giuseppe, and we went together to the gate, where there was a carriage with two horses and a driver, and we drove day and night without stopping except to change horses, until we got to Castelnuovo. We arrived at dawn, and were overtaken there by my husband.

She denied that Giuseppe was in the house when she was preparing to leave it, denied sending him any letters, or receiving any from him. 'I don't know how to read manuscript, and I don't know how to write.' This was a straightforward lie, and it is difficult to understand how she could have expected the court to believe it. Indeed, it is difficult for us to understand why (apparently) she carried conviction. But it seems that it was only the evidence of her sister Cristina Paperozzi that, later, showed that she had attended school. Browning certainly accepted the possibility that she was illiterate, and that her letters must have been forged by someone — probably Guido. There is nothing in the *Yellow Book* to suggest that she might not have been telling the truth — the evidence which reports that she went to school, where she was taught to read and write, is recorded only in the Cortona Codex.

Asked about the letters she had sent to Abate Paolo, she said that she had written at her husband's insistence – yet 'written' was scarcely the word, for 'as I don't know how to write, my husband wrote the letter with a pencil and then made me trace it with a pen and ink. He told me later how pleased his brother had been to receive a letter written in my own hand. He did this two or three times.'

She was shown one of the letters to the Abate, and confirmed that she had 'written' it as she had described. There seems to have been, at this stage, no argument whatsoever about the authenticity of the document, though one would have expected it to be perfectly clear whether the letters had been inked over an existing pencil text by a naive and inexperienced calligrapher. There is no evidence that the letters were examined, nor that anyone commented on their state – yet they were presumably produced in court; there is no reason why they should have been transcribed or copied. Altogether, both prosecution and defence seem to have been extremely slipshod where the manuscripts in the case are concerned.

Cross-questioned about the events at Castelnuovo, Pompilia repeated that she and Giuseppe had arrived at the inn at dawn, and had spent only one hour there: 'I didn't go to sleep nor lie down to rest.' Although a bed had been ready, she simply sat in a chair for an hour while Giuseppe arranged for fresh horses. Told that the innkeeper and servants had testified that she had slept all night in the same upstairs room as Giuseppe, she repeated indignantly that 'nobody can say so, because I didn't rest at all, and was only there for an hour'.

No fewer than six distinguished citizens of Arezzo sent written testimony of 'the continual scolding and ill-treatment [Pompilia] has suffered at the hands of Count Guido, her husband, Signora Beatrice, her mother-in-law, and Signor Canon Girolamo, her brother-in-law'. Conti and the priest Romano were among those who wrote of 'the public talk and notoriety' of the situation within the Franceschini household. Guido's uncle, Tomaso Romani, sent a letter describing how he and his wife had seen Pompilia in a distressed state one day at the Duomo, having fled there from Guido, and one Bartholomeo Albergotti, 'a gentleman', testified that he too had seen the girl at the Bishop's palace in great distress, apparently seeking Marchetti's help.

The court made its decision on 24 September 1697. Giuseppe was found guilty of having carnal knowledge of Pompilia, but no decision was reached about the accusation of adultery made against her – though it was agreed that she had certainly eloped. Venturini seems to have felt some sympathy for her, for he simply sent her to La Scalette, or to give it its formal title Il Conservatorio di Santa Croce della Penitenza, an

institution for fallen women in the Via della Lungara –
not as a punishment, but for her own protection against
Guido, who, the court recognised, was furious and
might try to harm her. (The courts often took such a
course in order to protect errant wives or daughters
from their husbands or fathers.) Adding insult to injury,
Guido was made responsible for her upkeep there.

The Franceschini – and Guido in particular – were
furious. First of all, the two judgements seemed
irreconcilable: if Giuseppe had been found guilty of
carnal knowledge of Pompilia, how could she be
guiltless? The insult to common sense joined the insult
to his honour and his fury at a result which placed an
impediment in the way of his securing that part of the
dowry which the Comparini still owed him (he had
petitioned both the government and the Pope on that
account, but clearly for the time was not going to get
anywhere). Abate Paolo immediately claimed that at
least Pompilia's parents should provide for her keep
while she was in La Scalette – but was told that if the
Franceschini family declined to pay for her food, 'an
unknown person' had offered to do so. We can only
guess who the 'unknown person' was – it may have
been a family friend called Tighetti, of whom we shall
hear more. But at any event, the very idea was an
additional affront to Guido's honour. The Procurator of
Charity suggested a way out: he would see that funds
were provided, and Paolo should repay the public

purse out of the money which had been found on Pompilia at the time of her arrest, which she had taken from her husband.

Meanwhile, Venerino, the driver, was freed, but the unfortunate Guillichini received a severe sentence – five years' imprisonment. Though he had played a very minor part in the plot to help Pompilia remove from Arezzo, he had panicked and fled the city before Giuseppe's trial – unfortunately first calling on Signora Contenti, the Franceschini's nosy neighbour, and threatening her with violence should she give evidence against him. Equally unwisely, he had allowed himself to be seen in the street carrying arms. So an example was made of him (though a few months later he was pardoned, and his sentence commuted).

The first flurry of legal action was now over. The Governor's court had found Giuseppe guilty, but Pompilia innocent, and had imposed sentences more in line with indiscretion than with crime. Giuseppe was at large at Civita Vecchia, where nothing would prevent him from living as frivolous and aimless a life as he had lived at Arezzo; the Comparini still retained much of the dowry which by rights belonged to Count Guido; Pompilia was out of reach in the Scalette; and Guido in effect had neither wife nor child.

Worse news was to come: too soon Guido was to hear that Pompilia was pregnant, and had little doubt that the child was not his.

# FOUR

# Only a Strip of Flesh

*Vengeance, you know, burst, like a mountain-wave*
*That holds a monster in it, o'er the house,*
*And wiped its filthy four walls free again*
*With a wash of hell-fire . . .*

When Pietro and Violante discovered that Pompilia was pregnant, they must surely have been suspicious. She continued to deny familiarity with Giuseppe, but whatever she said, the fact that after several years of fruitless marriage she should suddenly conceive just at the time when she was suspected of an extramarital affair seemed suggestive. Violante smuggled into her cell at the Scalette a number of specifics which her friends recommended as certain to provoke a miscarriage. They failed to work. When the girl began to show, and the pregnancy became obvious, the nuns protested that it would be quite improper for her to remain among them. On 12 October she was allowed to return to her parents' house. The Notary for the Poor recorded that Pompilia:

promises to keep to the home of Pietro (son of the former Francesco Comparini) situated in Via Paolina, as a safe and secure prison, and not to leave it, either by day or by night, nor to show herself at the doors or open windows under any pretext whatsoever . . .

A few weeks later she filed for divorce – or rather her father began proceedings on her behalf. In reply the Franceschini family started proceedings against her in the criminal court at Arezzo, charging her with adultery and theft and citing Guillichini and Rossi as accessories (Giuseppe's name was not mentioned). It was Beatrice who put the case in train – Guido had gone off to Florence to consult with the Grand Duke of Tuscany, Cosimo III, a former patron of the Franceschini family whose own frivolous wife, Marguerite-Louise d'Orléans, had abandoned him in 1675, and who therefore might be expected to be firmly on Guido's side. When he came home he found that his mother had collected together no fewer than thirty witnesses who were prepared to testify on his behalf – to speak of Pompilia's loose behaviour, the disgraceful conduct of her parents, the unwonted attentions paid by the priest Caponsacchi to the young Countess Franceschini. Finding so many witnesses had not been difficult: as Canon Girolamo put it, 'after the criminal flight, the whole town said that there must surely have passed some correspondence between them', and people began to recall incidents that seemed to support their suspicions. The point of the case was less to discredit Pompilia further (Guido had nothing to gain from exacerbating the scandal) than to obtain a verdict that might put pressure on the Roman court to make a similar finding, and speedily. Pietro was clearly determined to keep his hands on Pompilia's dowry, and if the court found in Guido's favour there would be more pressure on his father-in-law to hand over the money and bonds, while at the same time some of the disgrace and shame now piled on the Franceschini family would be shifted to the Comparini.

The Tuscan court had no hesitation in condemning Pompilia: Joseph Vesinius signed a judgement on 24 December 1697 which was sent to Rome for Guido's comfort. The continued absence of Guillichini, after his flight, very probably influenced the judge; the Guillichini family was extremely distinguished, and if one of its members thought fit to remain in hiding rather than to return and defend himself, there must presumably be a very good reason – his absence was tantamount to a confession.

The result of the case seemed to the Comparini, back in Rome, to be relatively unimportant – Pompilia was not about to return to Arezzo and put herself within reach of the authorities there, and as for the family's reputation, well, the damage had already been done.

Meanwhile, Abate Paolo was increasingly distraught. He was less and less happy about his involvement in his brother's messy marriage. It was becoming clear that the Church thought it highly improper that one of its servants should be intimately caught up in so scabrous and notorious a public affair. The Abate became depressed, sometimes to the extent that he broke down and wept; more than once he told his friends that he would throw himself into the Tiber. Matters came to a head when the officials of the Order of St John of Malta summoned him and informed him that he was deprived of his lucrative office as its Secretary. He immediately threw up his position as Guido's representative, sold all the furniture and books he had accumulated during thirty years in the city, took what remained of the money that had been found on Pompilia at Castelnuovo, left Rome for Venice, and thence vanished towards an unknown destination.

On 18 December Pompilia, seventeen years old, gave birth to a son, under eight months since her flight from Arezzo, but certainly more than nine months after what Guido now presumed was already an adulterous relationship with Giuseppe Caponsacchi. The child was named Gaetano, after the saint for whom his mother felt a particular devotion. The rumour circulated in Rome that Giuseppe had been seen near the Comparini house – that he had either with permission or without it come to visit mother and child before the boy was sent quietly out of the house to be cared for by a wet-nurse. In fact, records showed that he never left Civita Vecchia, some forty miles from Rome. There was, however, a regular caller at the house, a shadowy figure who has never been positively identified. In her will, Pompilia was to name a certain Domenico Tighetti as legatee – could he be the 'kind benefactor, moved to pity, and ministering to their aid' and the man who had agreed to pay for Pompilia's support if the Franceschini refused? If so, nothing more is known of him than the bare fact that he existed, and may have become guardian of her little son after her death.

In a place so rife with rumour and among people so fascinated by events, the birth could scarcely have been kept quiet. When the news reached Arezzo, it was the final blow to Guido's pride. He was sure that the child was Caponsacchi's. The Tuscan courts had supported his belief that Pompilia had committed adultery on the road to Rome, and there was no reason whatsoever to suppose that the affair had not started before the elopement – if only by a few weeks. Guido became, one witness asserted, 'utterly drunk with fury'. His rage against Pompilia and her scheming parents was even greater than his wrath against her lover. He began to plan revenge.

Throughout the preceding months it had not been easy for him to find a sympathetic ear outside his own house. He was not a popular man, and in a dispute between a beautiful young wife and a somewhat unprepossessing middle-aged man even those who might be expected to sympathise with a cuckolded husband had been sparing in their understanding, though he did not want their pity. He needed to vent his anger, and chose a confidant whose temperament and opinions matched his own – a 22-year-old man called Alessandro Baldeschi, known as Santi, who worked on the farm at Vitiano.

Baldeschi was a thug who had already committed a number of crimes of violence, as he was to confess at the end of his life. Completely unregenerate, he seems to have fanned the flames of Guido's jealousy against his wife and in-laws. Having listened to Guido's complaints against Pompilia and her parents, he was as free with outraged commiseration as he could tactfully be. He may even have encouraged his master to take physical action – according to the Comparini there had been occasions during their time at Arezzo when they feared that the husband might turn violent. At all events, when Guido asked for practical assistance, Baldeschi agreed without a moment's hesitation. Would he go with the dishonoured husband to Rome to seek out his wife and give her a good thrashing? Certainly he would. Women who committed adultery could expect no mercy, either from the affronted husband or from the law. Unfortunately, in modern times (it was claimed) men too often shrunk from the duty of severely punishing wives who did not 'act modestly and live honourably'. Immediate and public vengeance solaced those against whom a wife had offended: it 'quietened anger and destroyed infamy'. The rigour of the law had become obsolete, and a husband must take summary revenge or live in disgrace.

It may have been Baldeschi who first put the idea of murder into Guido's head – and murder not only of Pompilia but also of her parents. The Count was still fuming with anger at Pietro about the non-payment of the whole of the dowry, and his father-in-law's efforts to reclaim what he had paid. He and Violante were perhaps even more guilty than Pompilia in dishonouring the name of the Franceschini. Baldeschi, having made the suggestion, rubbed it in. Then he suggested that two men alone would be inadequate to discover where the Comparini house was, to watch the comings and goings, familiarise themselves with the best time for an attack, then secure the entrance while the punishment was applied. He could arrange, if the Count wished, for two or three other men to accompany them to Rome, men who would not shrink from necessary violence. Guido instructed him to do so and agreed to pay, though, as Baldeschi knew, his means were limited, so the putative assassins should be engaged at the lowest possible cost.

A few days later Baldeschi brought three men to Vitiano to meet Guido: Domenico Gambassini from

Florence, Francesco Pasquini from Monte Acuto, and Blagio Agostinelli from Popolo. None of them were as desperately criminal as Baldeschi had promised, but they were all prepared to help, though when it became clear that Guido had more in mind than mere corporal punishment, Agostinelli, formerly one of Abate Paolo's servants, was less enthusiastic than the others, and to persuade him of Pompilia's treachery Guido had to take him to his bedroom and show him the rifled strong-box and the glass that had contained the sleeping-draught. But he still seemed somewhat unreliable, and the plot to kill Pompilia's parents was kept from him. Indeed, there was some dissension about the necessity to kill the old people, but when Guido, encouraged by Baldeschi, explained the subterfuge by which they had deceived him, it was agreed that they should be killed.

Guido provided his fellow assassins with weapons, and the little group made for Rome, arriving in the city on Christmas Eve. They stayed at Paolo's house at Ponte Milvio, to which Guido had a key. He sent two of his companions into the city to watch the Comparini's house and note the comings and goings. The spies were clumsy about their work – later, with hindsight, a neighbour was to tell how he saw a suspiciously idle stranger sitting on a wall in the Via Vittoria, and another noticed the same man leaning against a wall in the direction of the Popolo, and another in the direction of the Piazza di Spagna, 'watching every moment the house of the deceased'.

Guido may have heard the stories that Giuseppe had been seen in the neighbourhood – and Caponsacchi's life would certainly not have been worth a *scudo* had the assassins been able to put a hand on him. But, of course, he was not there. An anonymous writer was later to suggest that Pietro 'was supplied with plenty of money by the generosity of some unknown person, possibly a lover of the young girl'. If this was Domenico Tighetti, as has been suggested, he too was lucky to escape the assassins – although Guido's wrath was focused firmly on his wife and her parents.

The assassins waited until the Christmas holiday was over, then at eight o'clock in the evening of Thursday 2 January 1698 they went to the Comparini's house. Guido set Agostinelli and Gambassini on guard to prevent anyone from entering while he and the others were at work. Agostinelli and Gambassini carried firearms; Guido and the other two carried only knives – a shot would be too quick a death for those who had affronted his honour. Guido pounded at the door. Pietro called out of the window to ask who knocked so late. Guido replied that he was a messenger from Civita Vecchia with a letter from Giuseppe Caponsacchi. Violante heard, and shouted down from the little drawing-room on the second floor to tell her husband to instruct the man to come back on the following morning – she and Pompilia were preparing for bed. Guido replied that he could not. Curious to know what the news could be from her daughter's lover and the father of her grandchild (for surely that is by now how she thought of him), Violante went down the two flights of stairs, along the passage by the tailor's shop, and opened the door. The three men rushed in, and she was immediately cut down. Pounding up the stairs, they broke into Pietro's room, threw him out into the passageway, and, despite his appeals to the saints for help, murdered him.

Hearing her parents' cries, Pompilia in panic put out the light on the stairs and hid under her bed. But Guido had brought lanterns (though it was illegal to carry them), broke into his wife's room, dragged her from her hiding-place, and fell upon her with a vicious triangular Genoese knife with a serrated blade that caused as much damage when withdrawn as with the initial thrust. He stabbed her twenty-two times, his foot upon her body as he tugged the knife from one wound after another, only to thrust it again into her flesh. Then he stepped back, and told one of his companions to make sure the girl was dead. The man lifted Pompilia by her hair and looked into her face. Yes, she was clearly dead. They dragged her body down the stairs, and threw it across that of her father.

By now the noise had roused the neighbours. Agostinelli and Gambassini had prevented any interference; the others now left the house, and the onlookers cowered back as the five men made off into the darkness. A neighbour, a locksmith, ran to the Piazza di San Carlo to call a corporal of *sbirri* who was on duty there with one assistant. The two men were highly reluctant to enter the house, where assassins might still be lurking. Eventually a certain Marchese Nicolò Gregorio summoned up enough courage to face the scene within. Violante's body lay in the hall; upstairs Pompilia lay across her father's legs. The violence of the crime was shocking: the place was awash with blood. Not only had the murderers defaced the dead parents and cut their throats, but they had done their work so violently that 'they had also cut through [Pietro's] head just where it joins the neck, so that it remained attached to the body only by a strip of flesh and a little skin'.

Astonishingly, Pompilia was still breathing. A surgeon was called, and a confessor – the principal of the nearby Greek college, attached to the Church of Sant'Atanasio in the Via del Babuino. Fra Giuseppe d'Andillo heard her confession while a surgeon, though despairing of her life, staunched the blood still flowing from her many wounds. There was no sign of the murderers, though near the bodies lay a cloak and a cap dropped by one of them (Guido, as it happened).

Meanwhile, the police had been informed, and under Captain Andrea Patrizi a posse set off in pursuit of the assassins. Pompilia, in a brief interval of coherence, had whispered that she had heard Guido tell one of the other men that they should make for the vineyard. That indeed was what they did. Guido had been so strongly focused on his revenge that he had made no detailed plans for escape – he had failed to obtain a permit for horses, for instance – and the five men left Rome by the most obvious route through the Piazza del Popolo by the Flaminian way, then walked and half-ran almost two miles to Ponte Milvio, where the road divided. To the right the Via Flaminia, laid down by the Consul Flaminius in 220BC, ran and still runs due north to Rimini. This was the road along which Pompilia and Giuseppe came from Arezzo; fourteen miles further, and it passed through Castelnuovo. To the left, the Via Cassia was the shorter route to Arezzo, whence it continued to Florence. In the seventeenth century this was the lesser used of the two. As the eloping couple had remembered eight months previously, travellers were warned to take 'the Consular road' rather than the Via Cassia, which was besieged by footpads and brigands. It was for those very reasons that Guido and his fellow assassins took the latter route. At an inn at La Storta, nine miles from Rome, they knocked and asked for horses; but the landlord, for whatever reason, refused them. Guido must by now have been bitterly regretting his improvidence in not having horses standing by – had they ridden from Rome, they would have stood a good chance of reaching Arezzo before any pursuers, and even if they had been arrested there, a Tuscan court, which had already ruled in Guido's favour, would have been more likely to be sympathetic to his actions than a Roman one.

Their slow progress, and the fact that Pompilia had survived to set the police on their track, made capture almost inevitable. At the vineyard a witness told the police that Guido and his accomplices had paused there briefly before continuing on foot in the direction of Baccano. Patrizi and his men followed. There was more news at the inn at La Storta. The police caught up with the fugitives at an inn not quite fifteen miles from Rome, in the Merluzza district of the Compagna. It stood alone in the middle of desolate country, on a hill from where the road could be seen in each direction. Not that Guido set a watch: he and his four companions were too exhausted and cold for that. They wrapped themselves in their cloaks and huddled together on mattresses before the fire. The police carried firearms, and the murderers put up only a token resistance – but even that cost Patrizi dear: he was scratched by a dagger, his wound turned septic and was infected, and he died a few days later. When the effects of the arrested men were collected, one of their cloaks was found to be heavily bloodstained, and in the pocket of another was a spectacle case which had belonged to Pietro, picked up during one of those strange aberrations which have so often condemned murderers. The case was mentioned, but never used in evidence at the trial, perhaps because the men's guilt seemed so transparent that no such evidence was necessary.

Guido and his accomplices were taken to another inn at Ponte Milvio where they were examined. Guido made no attempt to deny his implication in the attack on his wife. As they were being escorted back to Rome, Guido in a carriage and the others tied onto the backs of horses, he asked how they had been discovered. When Patrizi told him that Pompilia had survived to set them on the trail, he was 'so astounded that he was, as it were, deprived of his senses'. 'What, is my wife living?' he repeated, several times; 'Yes, sir, your wife is indeed alive', the officer replied. Guido realised, then, that if he had only made sure his wife was dead, the delay in discovering the culprits would have given him time to get home to Arezzo, and almost certain safety.

After the scene of the crime had been thoroughly examined, the bodies of Pietro and Violante were taken to the church of San Lorenzo in Lucina and exposed to the public view. By the Friday evening it seemed as though almost everyone in Rome had marvelled over the viciousness of the crime. When the assassins entered the city at five o'clock the news soon spread that the leader of the band was Guido, who claimed to be a bitterly wronged husband who had merely avenged his honour. They were taken to the New Prisons.

Pompilia, meanwhile, still lay at the Comparini's house, too badly wounded to be moved. It was clear that she was dying. Her wounds were fearful, and the surgeon, Giovanni Guitens – in the manner of the time – let even more blood. Those attending her were deeply impressed by the manner of her death, which took place on 6 January. Four days later, Signor Tighetti, appointed her executor, collected the testimony of those who had attended her on her death-bed. Fra Celestino Angelo, an Augustinian friar from the Church of Gesu e Maria, who stayed with her day and night, 'marvelled at an innocent and saintly conscience in that ever-blessed child' (as he put it in a signed testimony).

During the four days she survived, when extorted by me to pardon her husband, she replied with tears in her eyes and with a placid and passionate voice: 'May Jesus pardon him, as I have already done with all my heart.'

But what is more to be wondered at is that, although she suffered great pain, I never heard her speak an offensive or impatient word, nor show the slightest outward vexation neither toward God or those near by . . . I say further that I have always seen her self-restrained, and especially during medical treatment. On these occasions, if her habit of life had not been good, she would not have minded certain details around her with a modesty well-noted and marvelled at by me; nor otherwise could a young girl have been in the presence of so many men with such modesty and calm as that in which the blessed child remained while dying.

Other attendants were equally impressed by Pompilia's beauty and resignation: Fra d'Andillo, who had been the first to reach her side, spoke of her as 'the most exemplary and edifying Christian I have ever seen'; Fra Nicolò Constantin, Fra Placido Sardi, Nicolò Gregorio (who had been the first to discover her body), Dionysia Gideon, Luc Corgi, the surgeon, Giovanni Guitens, and his young assistant Battista Mucha all set their names to a statement insisting that they had personally heard the dying girl swear that she had never committed any offence against her husband, but 'had always lived with all chastity and modesty' and that they 'witnessed her dying the death of a saint'. Abate di Liberato Barbarito, a doctor of theology in charge of the nearby hospital of St Anna, himself confirmed 'the tenderness of her conscience' and claimed that 'during the experience I have had, having been four years Vicar in the Cure of Monsignor the Bishop of Monoploid, of blessed memory, I have never observed the dying with like sentiments'.

Pompilia died at sunset on Monday evening in the house in the Via Vittoria. On the following Wednesday her body was carried to the church of San Lorenzo, placed where her parents had lain five days previously, and covered with a cloth of gold, candles burning around it. A requiem mass was said, but so many people were excluded from it because of the crush that the clergy continued to say masses for the rest of the day, and still there were those unable to find places. The funeral ceremony itself was equally crowded and the streets outside the church were lined with people as the cortege passed by 'with funereal pomp as great as had been the horror of the misfortune'.

In his cell, Guido was confident that his actions had been justified. It was widely recognised that an adulterous wife should pay with her life for her husband's dishonour. The killing of Pompilia's parents had perhaps been somewhat rash, and it was even possible that he might suffer a short period of imprisonment for that act. The men he had engaged to help him might also receive some punishment. But he was in the right. No Roman court would condemn him.

# Noble Precedents

*Who is it dares impugn the natural law?*
*Deny God's word 'the faithless wife shall die'?*

Everyone presumed Count Guido and his accomplices guilty of the particularly unpleasant murder of Pompilia and her parents. The question, where Guido was concerned, was whether his excuse for murder was sufficiently strong. In Roman law – and certainly in the eyes of most Roman men – the killing of adulterous wives by their husbands was still not, under the right circumstances, regarded as a capital offence, so the case hinged on the question whether the murder had been done genuinely 'for honour's sake' – *honoris causa*. The decision was a matter for the court of the Governor of Rome, before which the five men were brought a fortnight after the murder. The Governor's judicial deputy, Marco Antonio Venturini, again presided, this time at a murder trial – *Romana causa homicidiorum*.

As usual, not only the prosecution but also the defence was undertaken by the state, the Advocatus Pauperum or Advocate of the Poor being paid for his work from public funds. This was the case even when he was not defending paupers, though he was allowed to receive a fee when the accused could afford to pay. It was a generous arrangement which gave a defendant every chance. The Advocate of the Poor had a considerable measure of prestige, outranking the Advocate for the Fisc, and might be a distinguished clergyman (though the clergy were in general debarred from appearing in secular courts). Guido's defence team was led by Advocate Desiderio Spreti, assisted by Giacinto Arcangeli, the Procurator Pauperum. For the prosecution Marchese Giovanni Battista Bottini, the Advocatus Fisci, appeared – a brilliant lawyer, good natured and amiable, transparently honest – assisted by the Procurator Fisci, Francisco Gambi, who had had a distinguished legal career in Genoa, Lucca, Ravenna, Bologna and Rome. Courteous, amiable and conscientious, he was as learned as he was diligent. The procurators were similar to attorneys in modern British and American law. They prepared cases based on the facts they were able to establish, which were then presented to the court by the advocates or barristers, professional lawyers who concentrated on the letter of the law and had to persuade the court on that basis. This was, in any event, the theory, though during Guido's case the four men seemed to be on an almost equal footing, Gambi acting rather as Bottini's junior than as an attorney.

The personalities of the lawyers are hard to detect: very little is known of them except their professional reputations, and even these details are sketchy. Both Spreti and Bottini had been appointed to their positions by the Pope from among the members of the College of Advocates. Spreti was much younger than his adversary, and though esteemed for his piety, was much less experienced. He was clearly at a disadvantage – though he was greatly helped by Arcangeli, his senior in both years and experience. Arcangeli knew the defendants well, because among his other duties as Procurator of the Poor he had to inspect the New Prisons and report to Spreti on the condition of the prisoners, making sure that they were adequately fed, had medical attention, and – if they died in custody – a confessor and a decent burial.

Antonio Lamparelli was also in court. He presided over an organisation called the Archiconfraternitas of Charity, responsible for the well-being of prisoners. Among his other duties was the defence of the accused in minor cases, and it was he who had defended Pompilia and Giuseppe when they were accused of elopement and adultery. Lamparelli had clearly believed in Pompilia's innocence, and was never to be shaken in that belief.

For the purposes of drama, Browning caricatured the lawyers in *The Ring and the Book*. In fact, they conducted themselves according to the letter of the law, and no one can read the court reports without coming to the conclusion that they were all extremely conscientious and thorough. Browning (as Judge Gest remarks) treats them with contempt and ridicule (see the Epilogue, p. 229). But it is impossible for us to see them clearly; they remain, alas, lay figures. Drama is lacking, too, in what we know of the conduct of the case. There is no dramatic cross-examination of witnesses (the place for questioning prisoners and witnesses was elsewhere – often the torture chamber). Guido's own statement has vanished, and so have the statements of the thirty witnesses which Beatrice collected. We lack the cut and thrust of argument in a modern courtroom. All we have are the speeches of the advocates – and those are often extremely turgid, for though present-day advocates and judges often quote precedent, the Roman lawyers of the seventeenth century seem sometimes to have done nothing else.

Roman law was based on the *Corpus Juris* of the Emperor Justinian (*c.* 482–565), who published the *Codex* in 529, codifying the principal imperial statutes in force at the time of his accession, and later harmonised the writing of the jurists and commentators on Roman law in the *Institutes* and *Digest*, the latter in fifty books of extracts from judicial records. The *Codex* was, of course, revised from time to time, and enthusiastically and thoroughly glossed by subsequent lawyers, every line and almost every word being examined and commented on up to the time of Count Guido's trial. So seventeenth-century lawyers faced a great mountain of legal texts in which, they must have felt, there was an argument to conclude every case, if only it could be found.

During Guido's trial, the advocates on both sides produced reference after reference from commentaries on the *Corpus Juris* and other codes of laws, treatises on the practice and theory of the law, arguments and opinion given by counsels in other cases, and from *Quaestiones*, or discussions of particular points of the law by distinguished past lawyers. As Judge Gest remarks, 'the painstaking industry of the writers in the collection of precedents and the minuteness of detail with which every phase of their subject is examined . . . renders their writings appalling in volume'. So we have on almost every page of the trial records references to Johannes Zeithoph de Jure, the *Praesumptionibus* of Menochius, to Bursatus, Farinacius, Giurba and dozens of other authorities whose names now mean little even to students of Italian law. Having done their preliminary study, the lawyers in the case came into court with a mountain of notes and with long speeches prepared in which to rehearse the course of events leading up to the crime and quote those authorities whose comments on the law supported the argument they wished to make.

The defence had the advantage of opening the trial, but the disadvantage of having to try to destroy completely the reputation of a beautiful, young, murdered girl, the description of whose pious death-bed was already well-known in the city – not a popular task.

Arcangeli got to his feet first. His summary of the facts of the case was clear and workmanlike, leaning heavily on the deceit of Pietro and Violante, which had already been proved and was common knowledge. He emphasised the fact that the couple had not only presented Pompilia to Count Guido as their daughter, but had set her down as their child in the marriage contract drawn up by Cardinal Lauria. As to the circumstances at Arezzo, Guido's attitude and behaviour had been entirely reasonable. He had certainly kept Pompilia on a tight rein, but it was completely false to suggest that he or any member of his family had ever reproached her for her barrenness. Merely because her parents had been rebuked for going about the town disgracing the Franceschini by their loose behaviour, Pietro and Violante had encouraged her to complain to the Bishop, to accuse her brother-in-law of poisoning her, even – just before the Comparini returned to Rome – to kill her husband, poison his mother and brother, and burn their house down to conceal the crime. The Comparini's behaviour immediately after their return to Rome had been completely disgraceful:

No sooner had these pseudo-parents returned than they declared that Pompilia was not their child, but the daughter, by an unknown father, of a washer-woman of the lowest class, and attempted to have the dowry contract annulled.

Arcangeli used the word *inonesta* – a clear suggestion that Corona Paperozzi was a prostitute, which was certainly not the case.

The Procurator was perfectly clear about Pompilia's relationship with Giuseppe Caponsacchi, whom he was careful to call, again and again, an 'ecclesiastic', the suggestion being that he was a priest and that for him to have been on intimate terms with another man's young wife was specially disgraceful.

Day by day her love for her husband decreased, while her love for a certain ecclesiastic increased. Things went so far that on a prearranged night, when her husband was asleep – and I wish I could say that he had not been drugged by an opiate she herself had procured – she eloped, first stealing her husband's money, and was subsequently imprisoned, her lover banished for adultery. Then she returned to the Comparini's home, and there gave birth to her illegitimate child.

The news increased the shame and resentment of her husband. His honour lost, this nobleman [Arcangeli was careful always to refer to the defendant as 'Count' Guido] was pointed at everywhere with the finger of derision – and this in a country where a good reputation is cherished by every man of good family. The anger which had been slowly increasing now roused him to such fury, his resentment drove him to such desperation, that he would have preferred to die rather than to live in such shame.

His mind bedevilled, he set out for Rome with four companions, and on the night of the second day of this month of January, under pretext of bringing a letter from her lover, he is alleged to have gone to the Comparini's house, to have cut the throats of Violante and Pietro, and to have inflicted so many wounds on Pompilia that she died a few days later.

Arcangeli laid great emphasis on Guido's emotional and confused state of mind. The shame of his dishonour and his passion for revenge had so affected him that after the murder, 'he failed to think of his own safety, but impetuously set out for Arezzo by the Via Flaminia, the direct road, and he and his companions were easily apprehended as they rested at an inn.'

At this point Arcangeli introduced the chief argument upon which the defence would build its case: that for as long as Roman law had existed, there had been indulgence towards men who 'wipe out the stain of their infamy with the blood of their adulterous wives'. He quoted a number of authorities: Giurba – '. . . a husband who kills his adulterous wife is not to be punished with death'; Caballus – '. . . if the husband detects his wife in adultery and kills her he is not liable to the punishment of *parricidium* under the *lex Pompeia*'; Farinacius – '. . . if a husband kills his adulterous wife, although he cannot do so without punishment, yet he is punished more mildly'. At this point the defence also raised a matter on which they knew that the prosecution would rely: the delay between the alleged adultery and the murder. Killing an adulterous wife in hot blood might be forgivable, but to do so in cold blood, after a delay of over six months?

You may think [Arcangeli said] that the laws which excuse a husband killing an adulterous wife taken in the act do not do so merely because he is moved to slaughter by sudden hot anger. They do so in order to allow the prosecution of a husband who may kill merely on jealous suspicion, when the wife is completely innocent. 'Discovery in the very act' does not, in our submission, mean discovery in the act of adultery, but discovery of the *proof* of adultery, on which a husband may safely act either immediately or after an interval. We submit that when a wife is convicted of adultery the phrase 'taken in the act' does not necessarily mean that there is an actual witness of copulation.

Someone killing in self-defence acts instantaneously; but injury to a man's honour is not something which, like some other insult, is over in a moment: it nags at a man, pricks him, goads him, until it has been revenged – indeed with the lapse of time the injury becomes greater. We must remember that the Trial for Elopement, revealing his wife's viciousness and adultery, exacerbated Count Guido's sense of shame; he already found himself denied the company of his peers. Then came the news of his wife's return to her so-called parents' home, to further infuriate him. We assert that *whenever* the act of revenge had been committed, it could be argued that the lapse of time is immaterial.

The defence did not argue that husbands should be allowed to act 'audaciously', outside the law; on the other hand, it was surely the case that actions like the accused's were necessary from time to time if wives in general were to be persuaded to restrain their lust and live honourably. This had been recognised from the earliest times – under the *Lex Julia* wives who polluted their husbands' beds had been sentenced to death. Indeed, in the Bible there were records of adulterous wives being stoned to death (he quoted Genesis, Leviticus, Deuteronomy, Ezekiel).

The prosecution will say that Count Guido might excusably have killed his wife when they were caught together in the very act of flight, in the tavern at Castelnuovo – that he delayed too long, and took his revenge *ex intervallo*, after an undue interval of time. But he could not have attacked his wife at Castelnuovo except at the risk of his life. Consider: he was alone, the lover, Caponsacchi, was young and vigorous and armed – perhaps with firearms. One of the witnesses referred to him, indeed, as a *scapezzacollo*, or cut-throat. Moreover, the wife – who has been portrayed as a timid creature – herself drew a sword upon her husband in the very presence of the officers who were about to arrest her. Only the quick action of a bystander in seizing it prevented her from injuring her husband.

Count Guido no doubt wanted to take action on the spot – as he was legally entitled to do. But that was impossible. Then came the Trial for Elopement, during which time she was in the custody of the court. Then she resided at the Scalette. But once she had left the monastery, Count Guido acted at the very earliest opportunity. In our view, this fact can be construed as immediate action, as though he had killed his wife in the very act of adultery.

Spreti now rose to support his colleague, repeating that there could be no doubt about the facts. He recalled to the presiding judge the Prosecution for Elopement over which Venturini himself had presided. It had been clearly proved, there and then, that Giuseppe Caponsacchi had 'criminal knowledge' of Pompilia, and there could be no room for doubt about it: 'their adultery is notorious here in the city, in the country of Count Guido, and throughout all Etruria'.

Should there be the slightest doubt in the court's mind whether Count Guido's action was pardonable, he would remind the Judge that in a number of cases it had been decided that proof of actual adultery was not necessary. The Royal Court of Naples, among other authorities, had absolved husbands who had killed their wives on suspicion of faithlessness. The court should not underestimate the damage done by mere suspicion: 'Fine natures, especially among the nobility, suffer deeply in such cases – suspicion is never from their minds, and continually oppresses them, urging them on to the recovery of their lost honour.'

He quoted a number of authorities in support of the Procurator's argument that while immediate revenge was certainly excusable, delay was not fatal to a plea against the death penalty. One case he recalled had involved a delay of two years before a husband's brothers revenged his honour, and they did not receive the death penalty.

I ask the court to remember that the stain of a wife's adultery is the most discreditable of all injuries. A complaisant husband, who does not act to remove the stain, is no better than a pimp. Moreover, the injury done to him besmirches his whole family. We need look no further than the case before you. When Abate Paolo, brother of the accused, was pursuing his brother's case in the courts, he was sneered and laughed at even by the courts themselves, and finally was compelled not only to relinquish an honourable post and leave Rome, but even to leave Italy, pursued by the disgrace of his sister-in-law's adultery.

The fact that Count Guido had engaged four other men to help him to his revenge should not prejudice the court against him: he had done so merely in order to achieve that revenge more easily and safely. Nor should the killing of his father- and mother-in-law be held against him. Their complicity in the adultery of their daughter and in her flight from the matrimonial home had been established. The bitter libels which they circulated in Rome had been repeated in the lawsuit they brought for the restitution of their daughter's dowry. They themselves were chief causes of the injury and ignominy which had so damaged the Count; he had ample cause to revenge himself upon them.

Coming to the end of his opening argument, Spreti now turned to the case for Guido's co-defendants. If the court were to decide that the main defendant should be excused the death penalty, the same indulgence should be extended to his assistants, he argued. Once more he produced arguments from a long list of authorities – Paulus Castrensis, Jacobus Butrigarus, Bartholomaeus Caepollo, Hippolytus de Marsiliis, Bartholomaeus Socinus, Petrus Paulus Parisius – to show that 'what is permissible in the case of someone giving orders is permissible in the cases of those obeying them'. The minor offence of carrying prohibited arms should be similarly excused, especially in the cases of Gambassini and Pasquini, who were both minors:

> Such, [said Spreti] are the arguments which we have been able to put, however briefly, for the defence of these poor prisoners. We are confident that the court, recognising the briefness of the time we have spent in outlining the arguments for the defence, will remember the advice of Hippolytus Marsiliis, that famous advocate: that every judge is obliged by his office to seek out, himself, grounds of defence for the accused.

The emphasis on Guido's offended honour as the basic motive for the crime was heavy and intentional; it was an argument every Roman man would understand. Similarly, the suggestion that Caponsacchi was a priest was a calculated one: there was little popular respect for the priesthood, and stories of cuckolding clergy had been common currency since Boccaccio and before. The main difficulty was, of course, the gap of months between the discovery at Castelnuovo and the murder. A man crazed by jealousy might have been expected to fall on the guilty pair immediately, and the suggestion that Guido had failed to do so because he feared that Caponsacchi might be armed, or (even worse) because he was afraid of his wife, was not one calculated to give the accused man a great deal of comfort.

Francisco Gambi now rose to open for the prosecution. From the beginning he sounded a fine organ note:

> The deplorable slaughter of the entire Comparini family, which took place in our dear city on the second night of this month of January, and the shedding of their blood, cries out from earth to God for vengeance upon the criminals.

It was now his turn to outline the facts in the case as the prosecution saw them. The emphasis was not so very different from that of Arcangeli and Spreti: he spoke of the 'contentions and quarrellings' which arose in Arezzo, but contended that these were after all no worse than was often the case among 'friends and relatives'. Then, 'enkindled hatred' grew between the parties, Pompilia fled from Arezzo, and, as was well known, vengeance was planned by Franceschini, who gathered a number of men together, provided them with swords and daggers ('prohibited by the Bull of Pope Alexander VIII'), and slaughtered the entire family – Pompilia only surviving long enough to confirm the circumstances of the monstrous crime.

Gambi turned immediately to the defence's argument that Guido's delay in taking his revenge should not count against him. For every authority that argued this, he pointed out, there was another that opposed the view – and he went on to quote from them, at length: Rainaldi, Sanzio, Laurentius Matthaeus. But in any event in this case there were aggravating circumstances, each one of which was sufficient reason to impose the death penalty:

> In the first case, the decrees of the Governor of this city forbid the assembly of armed men. The court should recall the words of the law: arms should not 'on any pretext whatsoever, in military service or for the execution of justice, be carried or still less kept in one's home or elsewhere'. What can Franceschini's pretext have been for approaching Rome carrying arms, and such a lengthy time after the presumed offence? Such an action itself falls under the threat of the death penalty; if the court decides that the murders themselves do not merit the execution of the accused, they certainly fall under that penalty on the lesser charge, for which death and the confiscation of goods is the punishment. Moreover, even if we accept the argument that a husband has the right to kill an adulterous wife, we must remember that failing to do so at Castelnuovo, Franceschini then appealed to the courts, choosing the legal way of punishing his wife and her alleged lover, before returning to his course of violence when, in his view, the punishment decreed by the law was inadequate.

Finally, there was the fact that the murders had been committed at the victims' house, to which the accused had gained entry by pretence. The court knew that it was the general view that such a crime was even greater when committed in the victims' home, which should be a safe refuge. Moreover, the murdered girl had been living there under the protection and bond of the courts with the assent of Franceschini's own brother, and murder under such circumstances merited the death penalty.

There is in fact no reason for continued debate [he ended]. The question does not arise as to whether a husband may lawfully kill the relatives, friends or servants of his adulterous wife, even if he suspects that they were complicit in her adultery. Pompilia was under the protection of the law, and that protection extended to those caring for her; to kill them was a capital crime.

As to Pompilia Franceschini's innocence, consider the manner of her death. She protested, in the face of the possible damnation of her soul, that she had not offended her husband's honour. Those who are about to die must be presumed not to be unmindful of their eternal salvation. As to her parents, it may be proved that hatred and enmity existed between Count Guido and the Comparini – but this cannot excuse him from the death penalty, nor can it excuse his co-defendants, for the law affirms that in premeditated murder the customary penalty must be suffered not only by the murderer, but by all those who aid or concur in committing the murder.

It was Advocate Bottini who now asked the judge to consider whether the accused men should be 'put to the question' – that is, tortured. They had made 'qualified confessions'; but had they told the whole truth about the planning and execution of this particularly horrid crime? Had Guido told his accomplices from the first that he intended to murder Pompilia, or only – as one co-defendant had suggested – to mutilate her? The contradictory statements of the accused, some of whom had confessed to the crime, some of whom had denied the conspiracy and alleged that the murders were a great surprise to them, might be disregarded; what was more, Guido himself had confessed only that he had given orders to mutilate his wife, to scar her face, rather than to kill her. Had he planned from the first to murder Pietro and Violante, or was their murder simply the result of sudden passion – passion aroused by the sight of the two people whom he believed had, from the first, turned his wife against him? If justice were to prevail, these questions must be adequately answered.

Spreti did not argue too strongly against his lesser clients being tortured, merely suggesting that the weight of evidence against them was not sufficient to justify such a course. It would clearly be to Count Guido's advantage if his co-defendants, under pressure, confessed that they had exceeded his orders, in which case he could not be held responsible for the deaths, at least, of the older couple. Guido himself should not, however, be put to the question. The late Pope Paul V, reforming the law, had made it clear in 1611 that the highest degree of torture should not be inflicted except when there were the strongest reasons to suspect the guilt of the accused, and when the crime was 'most atrocious'.

The 'atrocity' of a particular crime was by no means clearly definable. There were four categories: *levia*, or trivial; *gravia*, *enormia* or *atrocia* (serious); *graviora*, *atrociora* or *magis enormia* (more serious); and *gravissima*, *enormissima* or *atrocissima* (most serious). It was generally accepted that the judge in any particular case could decide in which category a crime should be placed, depending on the social class of the accused and the victim, the time, the place and the nature of the injury, the kind of weapon used and the part of the body which was injured. A crime which set a particularly bad example was considered very grave; one committed at night or in secret was more serious than one committed in daylight and in a public place. Poisoning was more serious than wounding with a sword.

There was another yardstick. In general, a crime was described as 'most atrocious' when it was agreed that, should the case be proved, the penalty would be 'worse than death – that is, mutilation or burning' –

the kind of punishment inflicted on one of the condemned in a Roman murder case, that of Giacomo Cenci, a hundred years previously. This case, notorious in Italy even to the present day, presents a caustic view both of crime and punishment; since the Cenci case there have been equally horrid examples of family feud and murder, and equally dreadful accounts of the justice of torture and execution; but none have had so strong an effect, and certainly at the time of the Franceschini case it was as vivid in the public memory as though it had happened the day before.

In 1556, Count Monsignore Cristoforo Cenci was general treasurer to the Apostolic Chamber and Canon of St Peter's. By his mistress, Beatrice Arias, he had one son, Francesco, born in 1549, who at the age of twelve and a half, on his father's death, inherited two palaces and an enormous fortune. From the beginning, Francesco was an unprepossessing character. When he was eleven, he paid a heavy fine for beating a friend so severely that he was seriously injured. Three years later, he was married off by his guardians to Ersilla Santacroce, in the hope of correcting 'precocious sexual tendencies'. The marriage survived until 1584, when Ersilla died in child-bed – a merciful release, it was generally supposed. In manhood, he was a large, muscular, not unhandsome man who terrorised the country around Rome, ranging about with a gang of bully-boys and doing more or less whatever he wanted. He lived a notoriously loose life, paying regular heavy fines to the Pope for this misdemeanour or that, frequently exiled from Rome (a sentence he simply ignored).

Ersilla had borne him twelve children, seven of whom survived – Giacomo, Cristoforo, Rocco, Antonina, Paolo, Beatrice and Bernardo. The boys were at first sent to school, then Cristoforo and Rocco went on to university at Salamanca. The girls went to a convent as children, but when they reached puberty they were brought home to live with their father, who by that time had grown tired of paying for his sons' education; their allowance was so niggardly that they were forced to leave their studies and return to Rome to live in their father's house on the scraps from his table. He disliked all his sons, but perhaps Giacomo in particular, who married young, without his father's consent, and was consequently deprived of an income and lived in poverty with his six daughters. Meanwhile, Rocco was exiled from Rome for a series of miscellaneous crimes, and took advantage of his father's temporary imprisonment to rob him (helped by his cousin, Mario Guerra, a priest). He was subsequently killed in a duel. Cristoforo was also killed, after a public fracas about his mistress, a notorious courtesan.

Francesco received the news of the death of his sons with equanimity, 'seeming almost to be pleased at it', as one authority put it. When Antonina was twenty-two, her father, ever searching for original sexual titillation, made a determined assault on her virtue. She appealed to Pope Clement VIII, who did not find it difficult to believe her accusations – only recently (in 1594) Francesco had been imprisoned in the dungeons of the Capitol for 'nameless vices', which meant sodomy (rather a fashionable offence; so much so that young female prostitutes were at one time instructed to stand half-naked on a particular Roman bridge in order to encourage the young men of the city to a healthier heterosexual life). He had been released on payment of a fine of 100,000 crowns. There was no reason to doubt that he might want to add incest to his other sexual experiences. The Pope rescued Antonina, married her to a nobleman, and forced Francesco to give her a generous dowry. Francesco's reaction was to hate his remaining children even more, and (despite the fact that he had recently been re-married – to a 38-year-old widow, Lucrezia Petroni, who had the reputation of being remarkably pious) to turn his amorous attentions to Beatrice, by common consent an extremely beautiful young woman. She fought him off determinedly, and when he virtually imprisoned her in her room, she tried to follow Antonina's example and petition the Pope. Unfortunately she was betrayed by a servant, the petition was discovered, and Francesco redoubled his precautions against her escape, arranging to take her to a castle at Petrella, near Abruzzi, some two day's ride from Rome. There, it is almost certain, he raped her continually. This has never been proved, and possibly from a sense of shame she never complained of it, but he boasted of it in the nearby town, she later asserted it, and from what is known of his character there is little reason to doubt it. Even his wife Lucrezia, who also lived at the castle, did not deny the rumours.

The caretakers at the castle were Olimpio Calvetti and his wife Plautilla, who lived there with their two daughters. He was young and handsome, a splendid horseman, with black eyes, beard and moustache, and it is not surprising that when Beatrice turned to him for sympathy, he was free with it. They soon became lovers, and began to consider a number of rash plans for escape – including poisoning Francesco (a proposition which they had to abandon because the suspicious Francesco insisted on Beatrice and Lucrezia tasting all his food before he ate). They also planned to contact some of the brigands who haunted the hills near Abruzzi to bribe them to capture and kill Francesco. Before they could do any such thing, Francesco became suspicious of Olimpio, and dismissed him and his wife. They immediately went to Rome, where Olimpio called on Beatrice's brothers and asked for help in rescuing their sister. Giacomo, Paolo and Bernardo knew the castle and had lived there for a time in conditions almost as harsh as those under which Beatrice was kept. They, however, had the advantage of being men, and though terrified of their father had been able to escape by acting together.

Bernardo was too young to take any part in the discussions, but his brothers agreed with Olimpio that their father must be killed. He was then confined to the castle by a bad attack of gout, and they decided that the most convenient way of disposing of him was to take him unawares in his bedroom at night, kill him, and throw him from the balcony into the kitchen garden far below. It seems likely that Lucrezia was a party to the plot.

Back at Petrella, Olimpio hid in a house below the castle walls in the small town, and made contact with Marzio Catalano, a sympathetic servant at the castle. On the evening of 7 September 1598, Catalano admitted Olimpio. The two men waited until Francesco was asleep, and crept into his room armed with a poignard and a hammer. Olimpio battered Francesco with the hammer while Marzio stabbed him in the neck. The two men then dressed the body and threw it from the balcony into the kitchen garden far below, where it fell into a decayed tree and hung suspended a few feet from the ground. The two men then went to Lucrezia and reported her husband's death. She raised the alarm, telling the townspeople that her husband had gone out onto a rotten balcony, which had given way. The body was taken down and cursorily examined; the injuries were explained by the fact that he had fallen into an old tree whose hard stumps had penetrated his neck and eye. The impression is that the townspeople were not especially eager to cultivate any suspicions they may have had about his death, and the body was hurriedly coffined and laid in the Church of St Maria in the town. Giacomo and Bernardo were summoned from Rome, but failed to go to the church to pay homage to their father, and showed no interest in arranging a funeral service. This upset some of the more pious townspeople, especially those tradesmen who had been particularly patronised by Francesco – and annoyed the clergy, who had to forgo the funeral fees. Talk began, and rumour eventually reached Rome. The police sent a physician to Petrella to exhume and re-examine the body. The injuries, they decided, were scarcely consistent with the explanation offered for Francesco's death, and when the balcony was examined, suspicions grew: the rail around it was intact, and while there was a hole in the floor, it did not seem sufficiently large for a body to have fallen through it.

Giacomo had meanwhile taken Beatrice and the feeble-minded fourteen-year-old Bernardo back to Rome, where in due course they were arrested and thrown into prison. At the news, there was a considerable stir in the city. Sympathy was at first entirely on their side – Francesco's reputation for cruelty and sexual adventure was well-known, and Beatrice's great beauty was on her side (the birth of her illegitimate child was initially kept very quiet). A simple application of the *strapado* (or cord) extracted an immediate confession from Giacomo, who threw blame on Beatrice and even accused his younger brother, who had known nothing of the plot. The two women, Beatrice and Lucrezia, confessed after enduring two days of terrible pain.

The trial was a short one, and the death sentence was demanded. The defence, led by a lawyer named Prospero Farinaccio (who had himself survived trial for sodomy), claimed justification on the grounds of Francesco's continual violence, indecency and incest. But there was no evidence of the latter other than Beatrice's word – and if every father was to be murdered for knocking his children about, things had come to a pretty pass. A guilty verdict was almost automatic.

There was a public outcry on behalf of all three, but not a very vociferous one, for the public believed that only Giacomo would be executed, that Bernardo would be released on grounds of his youth and feeble-mindedness, and Beatrice perhaps sent to a convent. Her plight had caught the imagination of the people, as indeed had her beauty and the very prevalent suspicion that her father had misused her. But the Pope was not minded to commute the sentences. The fact that none of the accused had actually killed Francesco weighed not at all with him: the family had ordered the execution of its head; such an action could not be excused. It is fair to say that Clement VIII was not an especially merciful pontiff. Not long since he had ordered the Dominican friar Giordano Bruno to be burned alive for doubting the Immaculate Conception. It may also be appropriate to note that the execution of Giacomo would have enabled His Holiness to acquire the still very considerable wealth – in money, property and goods – of the Cenci.

The sentence was a chilling one. The penalty for parricide – which inferred not only the killing of a father by his child, but the slaying of any close relative – had always been severe to the point of sadism. The *Lex Pompeia*, which had developed from laws promulgated by the Caesars, proposed that 'the criminal is sewn up in a sack with a dog, a cock, a viper and an ape, and in this dismal prison is thrown into the sea or a river, according to the nature of the locality, in order that even before death he may begin to be deprived of the enjoyment of the elements, the air being denied him while alive, and interment in the earth when dead'. Giacomo was not to suffer that fate, though on hearing the Pope's sentence he might perhaps have preferred it:

We condemn Giacomo Cenci to the severest torture and to the penalty of death, and that he should be drawn in a cart through the town to the usual place of Justice, his flesh to be torn the while with red hot pincers, and then to be knocked on the head by the executioner till he die and his soul be separated from the body; and the latter after being torn to pieces, to be exposed on the scaffold to public view. As regards Beatrice Cenci and Lucrezia Petroni we also condemn them, and order them to be condemned to the severest torture and the penalty of death, they, according to custom, to be led to the same place of Justice and there to be beheaded, so that they die and their souls be separated from their bodies.

Lastly, as regards Bernardo, there being just reasons moving our mind to pity, we order that he be conveyed in the same cart as the condemned to the same place of Justice, there to be present at the executions . . . and after let him be taken back to prison where for a year's time let him stay in close custody and in durance vile . . . and then let him pass to the galleys, there to row incessantly so that his life be a constant anguish, and death his only hope of relief. Moreover we condemn each one of them to the confiscation of all his rightful property.

The sombre procession set out along an artificially prolonged route through the streets of Rome on 11 September 1599, just over a year after the murder. The unfortunate Giacomo was in the first cart, which also bore a brazier to heat the pincers with which strips of skin and flesh were torn from his body on the way to the square in front of the Castello Sant'Angelo. The child Bernardo came next, trying to cover his head with his cloak so as not to see the torment of his brother; the executioners tore the cloak from him. Beatrice and Lucrezia shared the final cart.

The procession was a leisurely one: it was six hours between setting out from prison and the fall of the axe on Beatrice's neck. Giacomo was beheaded first, the agony of his skinned flesh mercifully ended by the axe. Lucrezia mounted the scaffold next; then Beatrice. She was the object of the most interest. Those unfortunate enough not to have secured places near the scaffold for the execution itself crowded to it after the executioner had exhibited her head to the crowd and placed it on a table next her body – where someone crowned it, pathetically, with a wreath of flowers. Bernardo, fourteen years old, had fainted several times while watching the deaths of his stepmother, sister and brother in the blazing heat of the sun, but was forced to stay by the bodies for some hours as a lesson for his uncertain future.

He was finally taken away, as were the bodies. The condemned had been allowed to choose their place of burial. Giacomo had chosen the family church, San Tomaso de Cenci, while Lucrezia was interred at the church of San Gregorio. A dense crowd followed Beatrice's body to the Church of San Pietro Montero, where it was buried, the head on a silver dish by its side, the grave sealed by a nameless slab. After a few days Bernardo was taken to Tordinona Prison, and there seemed to be some hope that his sentence might be commuted to mere imprisonment. Indeed, he was imprisoned in the Castello Sant'Angelo for three years, during which continual appeals were made for mercy; then he was sent to the galleys at Civita Vecchia. In 1609 a new Pope, Paul V, released him. He went to Sienna, married a cousin, had seven children and died in 1626. The family's property had been confiscated by Clement VIII, although some of it was sent for auction (on his behalf). Nothing is known of the fate of Beatrice's child.

The nobility of the Cenci family did not protect its members from torture and death, but it was argued that Guido's should – as a nobleman he should surely be exempt from infamous or degrading punishment. Spreti did, however, suggest that if torture were allowed, the court must decide on a lesser degree than the dreaded Vigil, which the prosecution had in mind. Bottini had a simple answer: the court was agreed, he said, as to the heinous nature of the crime. Moreover, torture was not applied as punishment, but in an attempt to discover the truth.

The court agreed. All the defendants must go to torture.

*S I X*

# The Strapado and the Vigil

A trip
*O'the torture-irons in their search for truth ...*

The procedure for arresting and charging criminals was well established, and had been followed after the arrest of Guido and his accomplices at Ponte Milvio. They were first briefly questioned, then taken to Rome, to the Carceri Nuove. Assassins were always brought before a judge for interrogation at the earliest opportunity. Their names, nationality, age and occupation were noted, and they were sworn. The proceedings were conducted without lawyers either for the state or the defence being present, lest there might be undue pressure on the accused either to confess or resist the charge.

As might be expected, some defendants protested their innocence so vigorously and against so little proof that they were immediately released. Of the rest, some confessed, some did not. Any witnesses to an alleged crime were brought into court, face to face with those they were accusing – though the latter did not have the right to cross-examine them. If a defendant refused to answer to the charge, or pretended innocence when there was clearly a case to answer, the judge could either fine him heavily or put him to the torture (women were treated exactly the same as men). It seems that there were very few cases of any importance in which judicial torture did not play a part, even as late as the turn of the eighteenth century.

This had been the situation for at least a thousand years, and it was to be 1780 before legal torture was abolished in Europe. Under Imperial Rome, freemen had been largely exempt from the threat of torture; slaves, however, were not – and since scribes and stewards were almost inevitably slaves, and equally inevitably were witnesses in many cases, torture was common even in civil actions. Priests and members of the nobility were exempt from torture, the latter privilege stemming from the law that saved St Paul from flogging when he asked the court 'Can you legally flog a man who is a Roman citizen and who has not been found guilty of any crime?'

Later, however, things began to change, and gradually it became permissible to torture not only slaves, but freemen who were of low condition or had committed a particularly dishonourable crime – and later still, even members of the nobility who were accused of such crimes as treason, or of any particularly notorious crime. (Some emperors, of course, used torture, sometimes for their own pleasure and outside the law.) Gradually, the rôle of torture became more prominent, and by the Middle Ages only members of the clergy were exempt. The Inquisition used it uninhibitedly, which led to a further broadening of the bounds to a point at which almost everyone went in fear of torture. In short, it became an accepted part of criminal procedure, and as such was approved by the Church in most of the states of Europe between the thirteenth century and the end of the eighteenth. It was not widely inflicted as a mean of punishment or by bullies who enjoyed the exercise; judicial torture was a means of coming at the truth, and was sanctioned by the wisest and most reputable judges, and by the Church (which saw the extraction of the truth as a means of ensuring the salvation of the souls of probable liars). The extent to which it could be used, and under what circumstances, provided rich pickings for lawyers who spent hours and sometimes days deliberating on particular cases.

Once a decision had been made, certain rules applied: a judge must accompany the accused to the place of torture in order to question him under duress. A clerk or solicitor must be present to record what was said, and a doctor must attend, especially in cases where the torture was expected to be severe. The questions asked must be direct: there should be no 'leading' of the accused. The torture should not cause death or permanent injury (though sometimes, of

The inn at Castelnuovo where Pompilia and Giuseppe were caught by Count Guido after their elopement. The photograph was taken in about 1900 by or for Sir Frederick Treves, author of *The Country of the Ring and the Book*.

The inn at Merluzza where Count Guido and the assassins were discovered.

The Pretura at Castelnuovo, showing the windows of the cells where Pompilia and Giuseppe were imprisoned.

Two travellers leave Rome in 1680, the Castel Sant'Angelo and St Peter's prominent behind them. This is much as Rome would have looked when Pompilia and Giuseppe departed down the Consular Road in 1697.

The Piazza del Popolo in 1669. The scaffold for public executions was erected under the obelisk, facing the twin churches. The Via Babuino leads off on the left, the Corso straight ahead.

A prospect of Rome in 1680, showing the Piazza del Popolo (left) with three streets leading from it – the Via Babuino at the top, then the Corso. The Via Vittoria connects the two, and is the fifth street along from the piazza.

*Pitratto de Sinfelitse, Guido Franceschini, il qnalefo Decapitato in Roma alli . . febraio 1698 .*

A sketch of Count Guido Franceschini on his way to execution, dressed in the clothes in which he committed the murders. Drawn by an unknown bystander.

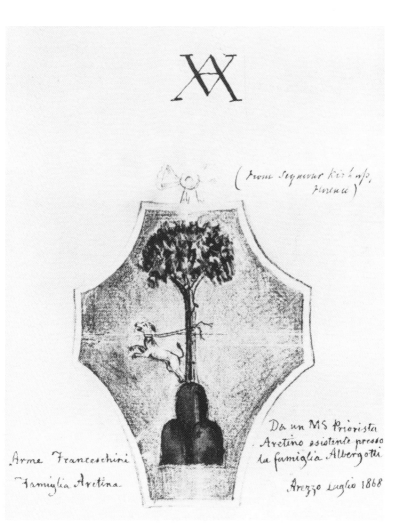

The Franceschini coat of arms, drawn and sent to Browning by Barone Kirkup, and pasted by Browning inside the cover of the *OldYellow Book*.

The third paragraph of an extract from the records of the church of San Lorenzo in Lucina, Rome, records the death at her home of 'Fran^{ca} Pompilia', daughter of Pietro Comparini and wife of Guido Franceschini.

course, there were 'accidents'). And the invention of new forms of torture was frowned upon: 'proper', tried methods should be used. It was also recognised that a confession extracted under torture was not in itself to be trusted. The confession must be repeated in court, and if the prisoner declined to do this, it was back to the torture chamber. If this to-and-fro continued, the judge must use his judgement as to the probability or improbability of the statement – whether the truth had finally been told.

There were two major means of torture approved by Italian courts in the seventeenth and eighteenth centuries – the *strapado* or cord and the Vigil. In each case the defendant was first stripped lest he or she might conceal a magic sigil which would negate the pain, and shaved – even of pubic hair – for the same reason (some sigils were tiny). The arms were then twisted behind the back and bound above the wrist, or perhaps about the elbows. The cord which bound the arms was fixed to a thicker rope, which was passed over a pulley above the victim. When he had been hoisted from his feet by means of this, the rope was suddenly slackened and he was allowed to fall – not to the ground, but to a point a foot above it, so that his arms were dislocated. If this failed, again and again, to have a result, weights might be attached to his feet.

There was an ingenious variation of the *strapado* which involved a sort of vaulting horse about six feet high, its back or body somewhat convex. The victim, his arms again bound behind him with a rope passing over a pulley, was seated at the apex of the curved horseback, with additional ropes passing from under each of his arms to the walls. His legs were parted and his ankles bound to a three-foot rod, which was then raised by a second pulley, so that his shoulders and legs were suspended in the air while much of his weight was still taken on the curved apex of the horse, pressing upon his buttocks. Victims were left in that position for many hours, even for days, care being taken that their arms were not too vigorously stretched, for men had been known to die before confessing, as the result of seriously dislocated shoulders. It was generally considered that there was no danger to life in this process unless it was carelessly administered or the person being questioned was too old or too weak to stand the pain.

The Vigil was feared even more than the *strapado*, perhaps because it was almost unknown for anyone to resist it. This means of extracting confessions is said to have been 'invented' by one Hippolytus de Marsiliis, who himself described it:

> It is a torture that does not injure the body, yet it is extremely efficacious, and if I had not made trial thereof, it would seem rather a joke than a torture; which is as follows: The defendant is placed on a bench

in a sitting posture, and there sit beside him two men to watch him so that he does not sleep either by day or night. And when the defendant leans his head to one side on account of sleepiness, the attendant on that side strikes him with the hand and wakes him and raises his head, likewise the other attendant does the same when the defendant leans his head over on the other side. When these two are tired and want to sleep, two other attendants are substituted in their stead, and these do not permit the defendant to sleep or rest; so that at the latest in two nights and one day the defendant will confess everything for the promise of sleep. And I likewise tried this in the case of two women criminals . . . who did not fear any other tortures, but under this in the space of forty hours they fully confessed all their crimes, therefore you may rest assured that this kind of torture is of the greatest power, and it does not weaken the body . . .

Ingeniously, some courts combined the *strapado* and the Vigil, stringing their victims up carefully so as not to injure them fatally; however, it was admitted that the agony involved was then so great that death could intervene before there was a confession.

The invention of printing meant that between the early sixteenth and mid-eighteenth century legislation and technical legal scholarship produced an enormous number of treatises, some new but many stretching back to ancient times; using this material, the courts could find precedent to order almost any accused person to the torture chamber. One custom general enough to be considered a rule was that judicial torture should be inflicted only when there was likely guilt, with the presumption supported by weighty evidence. The decision was, again, left to the judge, but he had complete autonomy. Judges could use their own judgement, and the more ferocious the judge the more likely the torture. In Italy, such judges were known as *iudices malitiosi*, whose malicious nature meant that they tortured vindictively and indiscriminately. There were many horror stories about these men. Venturini was not one of them; but he had no hesitation in ordering the torture of Guido and his companions – indeed, the law was such that it would have been difficult for him to refuse, although his decision was to lead to much legal wrangling about the resulting confessions.

Taken to the torture chamber, Guido, who had so far refused to make any statement that would implicate him, confessed at the mere sight of the ropes and pulleys – though he asserted that any gentleman, and even a 'common man', would have done what he had done to avenge his honour. If he had not confessed earlier, he said, it was only in order not to implicate those who had helped him. All the others also confessed without actually being put to the torture –

except for Baldeschi, who continued to claim that he had not been aware of the plan to kill rather than merely disfigure Pompilia, and that he had not had a hand in the murder either of her or her parents. The *strapado* was twice administered, and he twice fainted with the pain before adding his confession to those of the others.

# Trial in the Streets

*Earth was made hell to me who did no harm:*
*I only could emerge one way from hell*
*By catching at the one hand held me, so*
*I caught at it and thereby stepped to heaven . . .*

After the announcement of Pompilia's marriage, the Comparini's neighbours watched the domestic drama in the Via Vittoria bubble entertainingly along. Pietro was not the sort of man who kept himself to himself, and from the moment the banns were read Pompilia's engagement was the talk of the district. Pietro was well known in the local taverns, and freely aired his misgivings about Count Franceschini, while among her cronies Violante was enthusiastic about her daughter's prospects – a Countess at thirteen with a fine mansion waiting for her in Arezzo, noble grandchildren to come, comfort for the parents in their old age.

The pleasantly scandalous rumours about the problems in Arezzo after the marriage raised the temperature of the gossip, and when the Comparini returned to Rome, announced Pompilia's bastardy and then brought a suit for the return of her dowry, the uproar reached fever pitch. Then came the elopement and the resulting trial, the birth of Pompilia's child (and who was his father?) and finally the murders, the dreadful spectacle of the exposed bodies, the widespread story of Pompilia's death-bed assertions of innocence . . .

By the time the murder trial opened, everyone in Rome had taken sides. The feeling against Guido was strong. First of all he was not a Roman, he had put on airs that had been proved baseless, and to the usual prejudice against a 'foreigner' was added ill feeling against one who had married a pretty and popular local girl under false pretences. Then, the gap between the elopement and the revenge seemed unconscionably long. And his lawyer's attack on Pompilia's virtue was upsetting, in view of the fact that those who had been at her death-bed were completely convinced of her innocence.

On the other hand, there were those – and many among them had watched the girl grow up – who were not convinced by her death-bed protestations. Pompilia had not been especially popular among close neighbours. Violante's careful nurture of her daughter had given some people the impression that the girl had ideas above her station. She had married for rank and for money, and if money had proved short she should nevertheless have settled down with her noble husband, as many another girl would have done. It seemed that Guido would have been prepared to keep her, even after the revelations about her illegitimacy, which was positively saintly. His actions after her elopement were perfectly understandable. Any husband had the right to anger – and revenge – when his wife took off with another man. Then there was Caponsacchi: too handsome for his own good, and a priest, who should have known better. It was said that even after the birth of the child he could not keep away, and had been seen in the Via Vittoria several times after Pompilia's return to her parents' house. It looked very much as though the affair was continuing. And what *about* the child? Quite a coincidence that the wife should have conceived, after several fruitless years of marriage, just at the time she had taken a lover.

Little wonder that the trial was followed with breathless fascination. But there was a problem for the interested general public. While the lawyers' arguments and summaries of evidence were printed every night by the papal press – and are preserved in Browning's *Yellow Book* – they were distributed only to the judge and attorneys, for the use of the court. Verbal, second-hand reports of the progress of the trial broadcast in the taverns and over the dinner tables exaggerated and distorted the legal arguments until fisticuffs often resulted. Little wonder that, in the absence of daily newspapers to feed the appetite for salacious details of the elopement and more serious interest in the lawyers' arguments, someone saw an opportunity for profit. Presumably it was partly profit that led to the appearance of two anonymous pamphlets reporting the trial, but their publication may also have been encouraged by the lawyers on both sides – to have public support for their arguments might not (very probably would not) influence the presiding judge, but could do no harm.

So, halfway through the trial, the first of two anonymous pamphlets appeared on the streets. Printed in Italian rather than the Latin of the court reports, the leaflet was unsigned and bore no printer's mark – but there were rumours that Spreti and Arcangeli, the defence team, were behind its issue or had at least helped to prepare it, for it firmly took Guido's side. If that was the case, they lent their skill to the preparation of some 5,000 words of truth, half-truth, and downright invention. We can imagine that whatever the number of copies of the document printed, it will have been eagerly purchased and devoured (no other copy has survived, apart from the one tipped into Browning's book; both are reprinted in Hodell's edition).

The anonymous writer started out by denigrating Pietro – a lazy, habitually drunken man several times arrested for debt and married to an artful shrew with whom he hatched a plot to marry their daughter off to a wealthy man who could support the entire family.

The unfortunate Count Franceschini had been chosen. It was true that he had given a false impression of his fortune, but Pietro would have been happy to marry Pompilia to a much less wealthy man. He had been overheard to say, when someone had referred to Guido's relative poverty, 'Ho, ho! – it'd have been enough for me if it'd been half as much!'

The Count had treated the Comparini family well at Arezzo. One look at the evidence given against them by a single disgruntled servant was enough to show that it had stemmed from sheer malice – and in fact Angelica Battista had confessed to a number of people that she had made up all the stories of bad food and maltreatment in her deposition, just to revenge herself for harsh treatment from Beatrice. It wasn't surprising – who could seriously believe that a small suckling lamb could be made to last over a week as food for seven or eight people? It was all nonsense.

The trouble at Arezzo had originated entirely with the outrageous behaviour of Pietro and Violante, the pamphlet said. They had acted as though they were superior beings, had laughed at the Franceschini, had behaved scurrilously, had attempted to run the entire household as though it belonged to them. Yet when the parents decided to return to their own home, Count Guido had generously provided them with food and even money for the journey. The moment they got back to Rome their thanks was to issue the announcement that Pompilia was not their daughter, but the child of a whore.

The Franceschini family had every right to be outraged. Yet they still contained their fury, in the hope and belief that the fact of Pompilia's illegitimacy would entitle them to an annulment of the marriage. On legal advice they had hesitated to press for an annulment, which would not only have meant that the Count would have to return the dowry he had received, but that they must make public in Arezzo the fact that he had married the illegitimate daughter of a prostitute.

Meanwhile, the anonymous writer said, Pietro had had a number of scurrilous and defamatory pamphlets printed and distributed throughout Rome – some had even found their way to Arezzo – and had twisted and turned to prevent paying the Count the income from the bonds which had been granted to him as part of Pompilia's dowry. The Franceschini's patience in the face of all this was quite remarkable.

Then Guido had awoken late one morning to find that his wife was not in his bed, but had fled with his jewel-box. He suspected that he and the entire household had been drugged. Alone and unarmed, he pursued his wife and caught her at an inn with Canon Caponsacchi. He had been unable to avenge himself on them there and then: they were armed, he was not – Pompilia herself had actually thrust dangerously at him with a naked sword! Moreover, he was not at that point sure she had slept with Caponsacchi, and had been reluctant to offer violence to a woman he had so often held lovingly in his arms. So he had had them arrested.

But then the love-letters had been found in the latrine, the driver had come forward with tales of the fugitives kissing and cuddling in the *calese*, and the innkeeper at Castelnuovo had told him that the couple had shared a bedroom in which only one bed had been made up! And finally had come the decision of the court condemning Caponsacchi for having 'carnally known' Pompilia.

'Let anyone who has any sense of honour consider Guido's state of mind,' the anonymous pamphleteer wrote, with fine invention:

> Even unreasoning animals detest the pollution of their beds with natural ferocity, and not only tear to pieces the adulterer who offends their honour, but avenge the outrages done to their masters' reputations – an elephant has been known to avenge the adultery of his master's wife by trampling to death the guilty couple in the very throes of their passion!

Guido had indeed been delirious with rage, but for the time being had been comforted by friends who assured him that Pompilia's unfaithfulness would at least make it easier to divorce her. He returned to

Arezzo to lick his wounds. His brother, Abate Paolo, took responsibility for his affairs in Rome, but was so affected himself by the scurrilous nature of the whole affair and by the wagging tongues which associated him with his brother's dishonour that he even appealed to the Pope to intervene: His Holiness had found it impossible to do so. A little later, overcome by the scorn shown in so many of the faces around him, the Abate had thrown up everything, left Rome and even the country.

Pietro, meanwhile, was lording it around Rome on someone else's money – probably money given to him by some other lover of that notorious strumpet his daughter. In the taverns and streets he continually boasted of Pompilia's skill in deceiving Guido, getting away with his money and jewellery, and managing so successfully to deceive the judge in the elopement prosecution. The fact of her pregnancy did not affect him in the least, though Violante had tried desperately to induce a miscarriage, until the nuns at the Scalette discovered the truth and threw the pregnant adulteress out.

The news of the birth of Pompilia's son, no doubt fathered by the renegade priest, had understandably infuriated Guido even more – as had the fact, enthusiastically reported to him by his so-called friends in Rome, that Giuseppe Caponsacchi was continually to be seen at the house in the Via Vittoria, that he was 'wheeling round and round the walls like a vulture, waiting to put beak and talons into Pompilia's flesh, to increase the Count's disgrace'.

So, now scorned by his relatives and laughed at by his friends, he became completely drunk with fury. When, going to the Comparini's house, he found he had only to mention Caponsacchi's name to be immediately admitted, his anger boiled over: 'the dams of his reason gave way, and he fell headlong into the miserable ruin of soaking himself in the blood of those who had destroyed his reputation.'

There was no doubt he had committed a crime – nor that when he committed it, his furious mind was bereft of reason. But it was not fair to suggest that the interval between the adultery and the revenge in any way discredited his action: frequent and repeated insults had fuelled his anger and kept it alive.

The pamphleteer then produced a long list of authorities to defend Guido's action, including many Biblical and religious arguments to excuse a man who acted, even rashly, in a moment of anger and in defence of his honour. And finally there was an appeal to all right-thinking men in the city:

Count Franceschini should be punished mildly, as an example to immodest and impudent wives. Such women are not without supporters – they triumph, at this moment, publicly and privately throughout Rome in a treacherous coterie determined to oppress and deride those husbands who have any regard for their reputation – calling it affectation when a man simply wishes to preserve his own honour.

Some distortions of what we must believe to be the truth are obvious in the pamphlet; on the other hand there are allegations which it is now impossible to check – perhaps, for instance, Angelica Battista *had* made up or exaggerated her report of the Franceschini's meanness; there does indeed seem something absurd in the proposition that the whole family lived virtually on scraps. Were they really as mean, or as poor, as all that? Then, we know that Giuseppe Caponsacchi never attempted to see Pompilia after he had been exiled; this does not reflect particularly well on him, but it makes a nonsense of the allegation that he hung around the house in Rome waiting for an opportunity to swoop on her.

Needless to say, the prosecution team was not best pleased by the document. The Roman crowd, in general, was probably still on the Comparini's – or rather on Pompilia's – side, and while crowd opinion was not very likely to sway the judge; a result which was not only just, not only legally proper, but was also supported by general opinion, was much to be preferred to one that would provoke disapproval and possibly – in the case of a public execution –

demonstrations. A reply was necessary, and another anonymous pamphlet was hurried out, again without signature and without any publisher's imprint. There is little doubt that it was informed, if not written, by Bottini and Gambi. It attacked Guido even more bitterly than its predecessor had attacked Pompilia. It started with a positive fanfare:

> The notorious murder was committed here in Rome upon three wretched and innocent persons by Guido Franceschini, assisted by four men armed with prohibited weapons, who were brought together for that purpose by the influence of money and were craftily kept for many days at his expense.

The law prohibiting the assembling of armed men had been promulgated in the 1580s by Pope Sixtus V as an instrument against rebellion. A meeting of more than four men comprised an 'assembly', and as to the arms themselves, no firearm less than two palms-breadth long and no knife shorter than three palms could be carried – weapons smaller than these could be too easily concealed.

The writer or writers claimed that the sole purpose of the first pamphlet had been to try to rouse some compassion for Guido's crime, 'no less in fools than in the hearts of our most religious judges', and therefore to obtain a lesser penalty for him than the sentence of death. The crime had been the result not of an upright man's determination to vindicate his honour, but of sheer greed. Franceschini had been utterly determined to keep his wife's dowry, and had been driven mad by the lawsuits and consequent frustration which this entailed. That he was a greedy pauper was clear from the very beginning of his association with the Comparini. At the time when they first met, he had been staying in Rome, without a penny to his name, loafing about in the shop of a woman hairdresser where he was frequently heard to boast that he would set up house with a well-endowed wife. He induced the woman to find him such a wife, and she had introduced him to Violante. He had set about obtaining Pompilia's hand with all the skill with which Satan had induced Adam to taste the apple. He had not only lied to Violante about his income, he had actually written the lie down; and then, careful not to speak to Pietro, who might have been more suspicious, he made an agreement with her; and in turn she persuaded her weak-minded husband to accept the agreement – not only providing the Count with a large sum of money, but with a guaranteed income from a number of bonds. Pietro was forced to accept all this, and also to raise money on more bonds in order to pay the wedding expenses.

Of course, as soon as the Comparini arrived in Arezzo, they saw the truth – the Franceschini were living in penury. Not only that: they found that Guido had lied even about his family, which was by no means of the highest rank of the nobility, but distinctly second rate.

The Comparini's ill-treatment in Arezzo had been well described, the pamphleer said. They were ill fed, abused, locked out of the house . . . Then, back in Rome, after Violante had been persuaded by her conscience to admit the truth about Pompilia's birth, and when Guido's brother, Abate Paolo, had been invited to come to some compromise regarding the annulment of the dowry contract, the Count refused even to consider the kind offers of mediation offered by some of Pietro's friends!

Pompilia's sufferings at the hands of her husband were graphically described – as were Guido's plans to poison her, of which nothing had previously been heard. Charity and pity had persuaded Giuseppe Caponsacchi, a young man of the most perfect honour, to assist Pompilia to escape from the hardships and injustice of her husband's house; she had continually warned him against any supposition that she wanted anything from him other than platonic assistance. The flight from Arezzo had been direct and unconcealed. They had not taken some obscure by-road in an attempt to escape notice or deceive anyone – they had taken the main road to Rome. They had pressed on for many hours when they might have stopped to spend a night of passion together. The kisses which the driver later said he saw were a mere fiction: how could he have seen them in total darkness, when at the same time he was guiding his horses at speed over a rough road?

At Castelnuovo Pompilia had made a point of not asking for a room in which to rest, while Giuseppe had spent the entire time seeing to the exchange of horses. Her actions at the inn blazed with honour and truth:

> When this timid wife saw her husband, did she shrink from him? Did she acknowledge that she had sinned, that she had in any way forgotten her modesty and purity? No! Though only sixteen years old, she cried out against him for his abuses, for the threats and blows he had often given her, for the poisonous drugs he had prepared with which to take her life.

And what did the noble Count Franceschini do? Armed as he was with a sword against Caponsacchi's single, small dagger, he failed to take that vengeance which a justly injured man would have exacted. Instead, he ran to the police and had the two arrested – not merely for escaping from Arezzo, but for adultery! Yes, he was brazen enough to allege that Pompilia was an adulterous wife, and that he should therefore keep her dowry!

Everyone knew the result of the case. Caponsacchi had been banished to Civita Vecchia for a mere three years – scarcely the sentence that might have been expected for the crime of a priest caught in carnal knowledge of someone else's young wife! He had obeyed the sentence, and had never since left that place. Pompilia had been placed in the Scalette until she was removed because of her pregnancy, and a little later, having given birth to a son, this young mother was slain.

The writers developed their theme enthusiastically and at length: there was no proof of adultery, and even if one made allowances for Guido's state of mind when he found the couple at Castelnuovo, there was the fatal gap in time which made his crime cold-blooded and unforgivable. The matter of the letters was dismissed almost out of hand: they had been written by Pompilia – if indeed she had written them – not because of any love she had for Caponsacchi, but in order to persuade him to help her. He was not, perhaps, the most admirable of men; the supposition that a beautiful young woman was captivated by him was enough to persuade him to be sympathetic to her plans. But the letters – and for that matter, the conversations between them – were nothing to do with immodesty, or the flouting of marriage vows, or to give offence to a husband's honour; but solely to persuade a young man to help a distressed young woman. Finally, there were Pompilia's assurances, on her death-bed, that she was innocent of any misbehaviour. God had allowed her to live on for a few days, despite fearful wounds, clearly in order that she should have time to protest her innocence – and to condemn the murderers, for without her evidence the crime might have gone unpunished.

The rival versions of the affair circulated through Rome, adding fuel to the fire of argument. They remind one very strongly of the reports of notorious cases by the modern tabloid press – enough truth to make the stories credible, enough invention and falsehood to make them interesting. Nothing was made any clearer by either pamphlet; the public remained as divided as before. In the final analysis, the court had to decide. And the second half of the case was about to be argued.

# A Victim of Offended Honour

*Sir, what's the good of law*
*In a case o' the kind? None . . .*
*Call in law when a neighbour breaks your fence,*
*Cribs from your field, tampers with rent or lease,*
*Touches the purse or pocket, – but wooes your wife?*
*No: take the old way trod when men were men!*

If there had never been any doubt about the guilt of Guido and his accomplices, when the proceedings re-opened in early February the defence lawyers, faced with the additional confessions extorted in the torture chamber, must have realised that the result of the trial was even more obviously a foregone conclusion. The only course left was the one that had already been broached: the ameliorating circumstances of Pompilia's adultery. And the unfortunate gap between the time of that adultery (assuming that it took place) and the murder was very likely to destroy even that chance of the Count escaping the death penalty.

The prosecution was in better heart: the only argument they had to underline was that adultery never took place – that Giuseppe Caponsacchi indeed helped Pompilia to leave the matrimonial home, but that he acted just as the older and still missing Guillichini would have acted: he was merely an escort, and the fact that he shared a room with her at Castelnuovo was neither here nor there. Most travellers were used to sharing rooms and sometimes even beds with total strangers, and this could certainly lead to familiarity (as was the case until at least the end of the nineteenth century, as Casanova's memoirs tell us). But in this case there was no real reason to suppose that the eloping couple did anything but sleep together in the most innocent sense of the term – if they even did that, for Pompilia continued to deny it.

Opening the second part of the trial, Spreti immediately attacked the additional confessions that had been secured in the torture chamber. He quoted an authority which stated that 'when anyone should not have been tortured, and confesses under torture, such a confession is worthless', and took up again the argument that torture had been improperly ordered, since under the Constitution of Paul V it was to be applied only if the accused was under the most acute suspicion of guilt, and if the crime was 'most atrocious'. The argument sounds strange to modern ears: what could be more 'atrocious' than the cold-blooded cutting down of a young woman and her parents? But the term was, of course, a technical one, and there were sound arguments for Guido's right to avenge his honour upon the body of his wife, and for the court not to consider his act as 'most atrocious.' Spreti also argued that if there was some doubt whether an accused person would incur the death penalty, he should not be tortured so violently that death might ensue – and the fact that Baldeschi had fainted from the pain of two sessions in the torture chamber suggested that that might have been the case.

Guido's confession was in some ways useful to the defence, firmly underlining his one clear intention: to revenge his honour.

My wife's elopement was not only disgraceful to *my* house – it would have been disgraceful to any house whatever, even of the lower class. She left my home by night with the man Caponsacchi and his cronies. The driver saw her and Caponsacchi kissing in the *calese*, and they slept together in the post house at Foligno and again at Castelnuovo. And I have heard, since, that she had been equally loose in her conduct with other people, at Arezzo. . . .

Guido went on in his confession to detail the discussions he had had with his accomplices during their meetings at Vitiano, when they had talked merely of 'wounding' Pompilia's parents. After hearing about the trouble he had had with the Comparini, Baldeschi,

Guido claimed, had actually begun to seek the Count out, asking again and again when they were going to do something about taking revenge. He admitted that when Baldeschi asked if he wanted them to help him 'give Pompilia a beating' he had replied 'that she deserved not merely a beating, but death'.

Spreti was able to argue that Guido's confession, under threat of torture, made even clearer the fact that his sole motive for the killing of Pompilia was to avenge his honour – a motive that did not merit the death penalty. Yes, he had also planned the death of his parents-in-law – but as accessories to his wife's disgraceful conduct. Baldeschi, in his confession, had reported that Guido 'told us, in the presence of the keeper of the vineyard, that he had to kill his father-and mother-in-law because they had lent a hand to their daughter in her treachery – not to speak of wanting to have him, Guido, killed, and hoping to persuade Pompilia to do this'. No court should impose a sentence of death for such actions, Spreti said; and if that argument was accepted, torture should not have been applied, for it might well be the case that the court's sentence would in the end be less heavy than the pain already inflicted on the accused, which had not only been clearly unjust, but in fact illegal.

Bottini's rebuttal was brief. There could surely be no doubt in the court's mind, he said, that Franceschini's crimes were severe enough to have warranted torture in order to come at the truth. Quite apart from the treacherous way in which the murders had been carried out, the assassins had acted directly against the state – an illegal assembly of armed men had assaulted a young woman who was at the time under its protection. The truth was that the death penalty was thoroughly merited in this case, a fact which must have been clear in the court's mind when the order for torture was made, for if that had not been the case judge Venturini would not have taken that course.

After this preliminary skirmishing came the final arguments. Procurator Arcangeli led once more for the defence, and so much of his argument repeated the charges brought against the Comparini by the first anonymous pamphleteer that his speech underlines the probability that he and Spreti were behind the leaflet. He relied heavily on Pompilia's alleged love-letters to Giuseppe, scorning the suggestion that they could have been forged or that Pompilia could have been forced to trace them under Guido's instruction. Moreover, they were supported by Giuseppe's own letters to her. The correspondence taken as a whole clearly showed that the wife had fled from her husband for no other reason than lust for a lover. A fellow priest, Canon Conti – a relative of Count Guido – could not be regarded as entirely blameless in the matter: he had acted as a go-between, and there was some reason to suppose he was more than that. (By now, Conti was in no position to

come to court to resist such a charge: he had died, at
Arezzo, in the last days of January.)

> Any threats made by Count Guido against his wife were
> made in an attempt to preserve his honour – and his wife
> could at any time have freed herself from such threats
> without making a scandal, without fleeing from Arezzo,
> and without shame, simply by living a chaste life.
> However, she chose otherwise: too prone to the tickling
> of the flesh, she set aside everything but the fulfilment of
> her beastly desires, without any respect for her marriage
> vows. It would be foolish to doubt this in the face of the
> evidence set out in the prosecution for Elopement, and
> indeed from the tender love-letters she sent to
> Caponsacchi . . . Equally, no one could be so senseless
> and weak-minded as not to believe that when they were
> found together at the inn, they had not been intimate.
> Remember Pompilia's lie about the time they arrived at
> that inn. If she had done no evil, why should she lie?

Once again, Guido's failure to attack Giuseppe there
and then was excused on the grounds of his relative
weakness and lack of arms; and again and again the
theme of honour revenged was pressed home. In his
peroration, Arcangeli pulled out all the stops:

> Count Guido killed in order that his honour, which had
> been buried in infamy, might rise again. He killed his

wife, who had been his shame, and her parents, who had set aside all truth, repudiated their daughter, and piled further disgrace on him by publicly declaring that she was the daughter of a harlot. They perverted her mind, and not only pimped for her, but actually compelled her to indulge in illicit amours.

Count Guido did what he did in order to escape a life of disgrace, a life in which he was now loathed by his relatives, sneered at by the nobility, abandoned by his friends, a figure of fun to all Arezzo. He killed his wife in her own home so that the adulteress and her parents should know that no refuge was safe from one whose honour had been wounded. He killed them lest even more shameful deeds should continue within those walls, and so that the home which had witnessed such deeds should also witness their punishment. He killed them because in no other way could his reputation, so monstrously wounded, be healed. He killed them as a warning to all wives that the sacred laws of marriage should be religiously kept. He killed them, finally, that he might either regain an honourable place among men, or at least might fall the pitied victim of his own offended honour.

Spreti, the Advocate, followed his colleague, but spoke more briefly. He too insisted that the confessions extracted under torture should be ignored, and once again suggested that the fact that the murders were done in the cause of honour excused Guido from the death penalty; he quoted additional authorities in support of his argument. Yet again there was an emphasis on the manner of the escape, the love-letters, the alleged illicit amours at Castelnuovo. But he did turn, for a couple of paragraphs, to Guido's accomplices, who for the most part had gone unmentioned during the legal arguments. Agostinelli had confessed under torture, but only to being present while the murders were done, and not to assisting with them. Spreti believed that Gambassini and Pasquini were under the age at which the death penalty could be applied, but this was a matter for the prosecution, and neither Bottini nor Gambi had provided any proof that seriously implicated them.

Bottini's enormously lengthy and comprehensive reply for the prosecution was generally considered to be a masterpiece of argument. In his opening paragraph he again firmly demanded the death penalty, and scorned the defence's arguments for leniency. The excuse that Guido had killed in defence of his honour had no foundation in fact and was irrelevant in law.

If a woman were caught *in flagrante* or obviously preparing to betray her husband, then a man could perhaps be forgiven for sudden and fatal anger, and the penalty for her murder might be mitigated, depending on the circumstances. But it is absolutely certain that in order to escape the death penalty, the mere suspicion of adultery is not enough. The clearest proof is necessary – for example, the confession of the wife.

Such proof is entirely lacking in this case. The unfortunate wife continually denied adultery – until her last breath, as those who tended her death-bed have asserted. Not only that, but she did not confess adultery as a sin in her last confession; and we must give that fact weight, for no one can be presumed to die unmindful of their eternal safety.

He then turned to the awkward question of the earlier court's condemnation of Giuseppe for 'criminal knowledge' of Pompilia during the elopement. It could be argued – and he did argue – that the prosecution had in fact failed to prove the charge of 'criminal knowledge'. The court had not found Pompilia guilty of undue familiarity with the man who had helped her to escape, and clearly the crime of adultery was indivisible: whatever the verdict against him, Guido could not be found guilty and Pompilia innocent!

Moreover, Caponsacchi was condemned merely to three years' banishment – the mildest possible sentence, which cannot correspond with the offences of running away with a married woman and having carnal knowledge of her. A far stricter penalty would have been inflicted for proven adultery. In this case, notorious adultery has clearly not been proved; and just as public vengeance, which is to be decreed by a judge, cannot be based upon it, so private vengeance cannot be excused when it is taken by a husband who murders a wife in cold blood after an interval of time.

Bottini was particularly scathing about the letters produced by the defence in the earlier trial, and exhibited again in the present case – especially the one alleged to have been written by Pompilia to Abate Paolo, in which she had 'confessed' that her parents had urged her to poison the entire Franceschini family and burn the house down afterwards:

There cannot be a better negation of such a document than its very tone – than the inclusion of words so improbable that no judge could believe them. Who could be so ignorant of the duty of child to parents as to believe that an adolescent, not more than fourteen years of age, married away from her father's home, grieving bitterly for the absence of her parents, living wretchedly in her husband's house – so wretchedly that she was forced to appeal to the Bishop and the Governor about conditions there – could have written in such terms to her husband's brother, who had himself shown no sympathy to her, reporting such evil commands? Unless, indeed, she was forced by her husband to write the letter in order that it might be used against her family.

And if her husband demanded that she write such a letter, could such a child refuse to do it? Merely to read the document is to feel a thrill of horror at the compulsion she was under.

The supposed love-letters to Caponsacchi might not have been written or dictated by the husband – indeed, it seemed improbable; but it was equally improbable that they were written by Pompilia, whose claim to be illiterate was well supported. The fact that she was able to write to her parents from prison at Castelnuovo proved nothing; in extreme circumstances, people had been known to acquire such skills as writing in a very short time. And was it likely that so young a girl possessed the classical knowledge to write of herself as Amarillis, Dorinda, Lilla, Ariadne, or refer to a lover as Ilago or Fedone? Would Pompilia have written such lascivious phrases as 'Venus in fashioning you took the measure of your limbs with her own girdle'? The identity of the writer of the letters would probably remain forever a mystery – they might have been written at Guido's instigation by someone whose connection with the crime remained unknown.

Of course, Bottini continued, it would have been better had Pompilia appealed again to the Bishop or to the Lord Governor for sanctuary rather than escaping in the manner she chose. But it must be remembered that she had, indeed, already appealed to both – and had received short shrift. It would have been better, then, had she asked a servant to accompany her. The defence was quite right to suggest this.

But the fear of impending danger does not encourage one to look patiently for good counsel – and this may be especially true of a wretched young wife, destitute of all aid and exposed to the anger of a husband and mother-in-law. Two men – relatives of her husband – had encouraged her to escape, and it is unthinkable that they would have conspired against Franceschini's honour without the strongest reason, and without confidence in Caponsacchi's honesty and modesty. One of the two men, Gregorio Guillichini, had indeed offered to accompany Pompilia to Rome, and would have done so had not illness intervened.

There was no question that Pompilia believed that Caponsacchi would behave himself during their journey together. The slightest undue familiarity in his letters to her had been rebuked – when, in one, he had overstepped the mark, she had immediately accused him of immodesty; if she herself had seemed to use strong language, it had been in order to persuade him to help her. The letters, even if they had been written by her, were not an invitation to adultery – and the alleged proofs of infidelity at Arezzo were so weak as to be negligible. The single witness who had given evidence that she had seen Caponsacchi enter and leave Guido's house had been shown to be disreputable and dishonest. The driver who alleged improper behaviour during the flight could not be believed. Bottini repeated the argument of the second anonymous pamphleteer: 'How, when the witness was intent on driving the carriage with such great speed as to appear to be flying (as some onlooker put it) could he have looked behind him and seen his passengers kissing without causing a disaster? – even if it had not been almost entirely dark?'

The alleged adultery at Castelnuovo was equally unproven. Caponsacchi had confessed merely to having rested for a while, lying fully clothed on a bed, in the same room as Pompilia. She had denied any familiarity. The court should remember that some authorities had claimed that even should a young man be seen alone and naked in the same room as a woman, adultery could not be assumed, but merely the possible preparation for it. Nor should adultery be assumed just because a servant had been ordered to prepare only one of two beds in a bedroom. It did not follow that both parties slept in it. As for Pompilia's indiscretion in stating that they had arrived at the inn at dawn when in fact they had spent the night there – that was indeed merely an indiscretion, the result of her desire to escape any accusation of immodesty.

Even lacking proof of adultery, the court might think there would have been some excuse for Guido's action had he fallen on the couple and killed them at the inn at Castelnuovo. But he had not – and his excuse was that Caponsacchi was young, violent and more fully armed. But no authority claimed that vengeance on a wife's lover should be delayed because its execution might put the husband in danger! – and in any event, he could have rushed upon his wife the moment that she had been disarmed and Caponsacchi arrested. Moreover, 'he would not have taken such care of his own safety if his honour had been so fatally stung – just anger knows no moderation.'

Whatever anyone might feel about the murder of a wife whose actions had admittedly been unwise, there could be no excuse for the barbarous slaughter of her parents, Bottini said. In his confession, Franceschini attempted to involve them in the debasement of his honour by speaking of their part in his wife's flight and alleged adultery. But there had been no proof of this; and the accused's brother, Abate Paolo, had assented to Pompilia being placed in their care after her release from the Scalette. Would he have done this if he had believed that Pietro and Violante had encouraged her disobedience?

It had been argued that because Violante had opened the door to the murderers on hearing Caponsacchi's name, she was ready to encourage his continued intimacy with her daughter. But how strange it would have been for the mother not to have welcomed to her house the man who had cared for her daughter on the arduous journey from her husband's house to her parents' hearth! The accusation that he had been familiar with Pompilia in the weeks before the murder could only be described as absurd, for during that time he had been forty miles away at Civita Vecchia, and there was no evidence that he had ever left that place.

No, the true reason for the murder of Pietro and Violante had been hatred, pure and simple – hatred because of the revelation of Pompilia's illegitimacy, which had deprived Count Franceschini of a fat dowry and inheritance, and because of the Comparini's stories of his family's meanness and the wretched conditions in which they lived.

It might be argued that the accused had a right to be angry at the part Pompilia's parents had played in persuading her to leave his house. But there was no proof whatsoever that they had done so. Indeed, if Guido himself believed this, why had he not entered their names in the Prosecution for Elopement? There was much more: argument against the assassins for bearing arms, for gathering together to plan murder – all of which was punishable by death – and for violating the home to which Pompilia had been released by the state for safe keeping.

Spreti's closing speech for the defence was a short one, almost giving the impression that he believed the case to be already over. He repeated again the earlier court's condemnation of Caponsacchi for 'criminal knowledge' of Pompilia, and insisted once more that whatever the prosecution might say, those words meant what they said. Yes, the penalty imposed had been very light – yet it had *been* a penalty, and the judges had clearly believed that adultery had been proved.

'Who can deny,' he asked, 'that Count Guido, reading the court's decision, should not have been angered by the public assertion of his wife's betrayal? Who can deny that he should be excused if he later took vengeance for such a violation of his honour?'

Pompilia had denied committing adultery. But she would, would she not? How believable was the word of a wife convicted of adultery, and indeed sent to a nunnery because of it? Even her death-bed denials should not necessarily be believed: 'she who lives badly, dies badly.' If Count Guido had some excuse for killing his wife, Spreti said, that excuse must extend to the death of her parents, who had so clearly deceived him and encouraged her. Should the court take the view that the deep offence to his honour, which had had the effect of unseating his mind, justified Count Guido's actions against his wife and her parents, that justification should excuse him from any penalty regarding the offence of bearing arms, or indeed any other offence connected with his action – for if the action itself was excused, so were allied actions.

Spreti's main plea was for Gambassini and Pasquini, though he reminded the court that Agostinelli had confessed only to being present at the scene of the crime. These men were, in the first place, foreigners, and not bound by Roman law. Moreover, Gambassini was a minor, and the defence could now produce Pasquini's baptismal record, which showed him also to be under twenty-five years old, and therefore also liable only to a lesser punishment than death. It was true that the judge had discretion where such leniency was concerned; but custom was very much on the side of indulgence, especially when younger men were in the presence of older men, who might be presumed to have influenced and corrupted them.

He turned back to Guido for the closing words of his defence, and of the trial itself:

> I ask the court to take notice of the state of himself and his noble family. The ignominy brought upon them by Pompilia and her family will give them cause to mourn until the last breath in their bodies – at least one member of the family has been in danger of losing his reason because of it.

A final appeal was drafted by another lawyer, Dionisio Pignatelli. He produced no new legal arguments, but decorated them with generous Biblical quotations as well as yet more ancient authorities for wife-slaying when 'horns were placed upon an honourable husband on a high hill in the eyes of all'.

On 18 February 1698 the judge gave his verdict. Guido and his accomplices were, as everyone must have expected, found guilty. Those who had argued for leniency were disappointed. All the defendants must suffer death.

Guido was seen to sigh heavily as he heard the sentence. He said only a few words:

> I feared a heavy sentence, but not that of death. My crime is great, but love of honour has blinded me to the fact until now that I hear the sentence. I appeal only to God. Without His will I would never have reached this awful pass, and I trust that by resigning myself to that will I may gain the merit of His pardon.

## NINE

# The Rope and the Guillotine

*'Pompilia, will you let them murder me?'*

The immediate response of the defence to the death sentence on Guido was to appeal to the Pope. The confederates cannot have hoped much from the Jesuit Innocent XII. The Pontiff was not only head of the Church, but also head of State, and in that capacity had to enforce the law. This was not an easy task in Rome, which was one of the most dangerous cities in Europe – during 1691, seven years earlier, there had been 180 murders within the walls. From the very beginning of his reign this Pope had been intransigent in his treatment of criminals – apart from anything else, the beleaguered citizens had insisted on it – and he dismissed the appeals of Guido and his ruffians almost out of hand. It was argued that Guido held a minor clerical office, and holding an office in the Church relieved men from execution except in exceptional circumstances. Two friends of Guido's wrote to Monsignore Francesco Cencini, a Florentine lawyer, asking him to send urgently proofs of his 'well-known clericate'. The 'proofs' did not arrive in time, but in any case he was merely a sub-deacon, and no more a cleric than Giuseppe Caponsacchi. His Holiness no doubt considered the question of the age of two of the other condemned men, but in the end ratified the death sentences, and ordered execution for the following morning. He was not considered a cruel man, and such haste was uncharacteristic: 'He was moved to this by the fear lest, during such a delay, letters might come . . . to save the life of Guido Franceschini, and that with such an example not only Romans but foreigners might attempt to commit acts similar to that of Franceschini, who had come into Rome from a foreign state with armed men in order to commit such a deed.' He may also have been moved by the fact that he knew the Comparini, or at least knew of them; Pietro had received several favours and a small pension from the Pope.

The executions took place in public on 22 February 1698 (the day after sentence was passed) in the Piazza del Popolo. Rome adopted a carnival spirit for the occasion. Public executions were still commonplace in the seventeenth century, and were to remain so for well over a hundred years – Byron was to attend one in Rome in 1817, and Dickens much later. They were an enormous attraction, and while authority may have justified them on grounds of example, the public regarded them for the most part as entertainment – horrid, perhaps, but no less enjoyable, giving the onlookers a highly acceptable *frisson* of sadistic pleasure. Punishments took place from time to time in other parts of the city: floggings, for instance, were often staged in the Piazza Navona; but executions usually took place in either the Campo di Fiori or the Piazza del Popolo, which was otherwise used partly as a marketplace and partly as pasture for goats – grass grew thickly over much of it.

The piazza was crowded long before two o'clock, the time set for the execution. A scaffold had been set up directly in front of the obelisk which is still at its centre, the block set higher than the gallows which flanked it on either side. Dickens saw just such a setting in Rome a century and a half later, the scaffold 'an untidy, unpainted, uncouth, crazy-looking thing . . . some seven feet high, perhaps: with a tall, gallows-shaped frame riding above it, in which was the knife, charged with a ponderous mass of iron, all ready to descend, and glittering brightly in the morning sun . . .' Stands had been erected and decorated with ribbons and garlands, their fronts hung with tapestries. Seats in them cost five *scudi*, or about £106 in modern currency. No doubt they fetched more on a hastily organised black market.

By mid-morning the steps of the churches of Santa Maria dei Miracoli and Santa Maria di Monte Santo – built only thirty years before the murder, and facing the scaffold – were crowded with onlookers, and those carriages which had arrived early enough to be allowed into the piazza were in danger of toppling under the weight of the people clinging to the sides facing the scaffold. 'The windows and balconies of the square were occupied by princes, ladies and cavalieri so that one could not throw there, so to speak, a bag of grain', a reporter recorded. Every place had been sold the day before the morning of the execution – some for as much as 10 *scudi* per person. One or two houses which happened to be unoccupied were rented for a whole year by astute *entrepreneurs*, the tenants making a considerable profit just on that one morning. Intrepid men and women had climbed onto the very roofs around the piazza, and when they craned their heads they could see that the three streets leading south – the Via di Ripetta, the Strada Paulina and the Corso itself – were entirely blocked with people as far as the eye could see.

Signor Ciccaprovi, a man in charge of arrangements for executions, meanwhile told the sacristans who attended the prison to make sure the chapel there was in order, and at two o'clock in the morning Guido and his accomplices were awakened. Had the decision been made, he asked? Was he to go to the galleys? He was told to get dressed because he was to be moved to another prison. The excuse seemed ridiculous; he guessed immediately that his appeal had failed. The four men were taken to the chapel, where confessors were waiting, having come from the Oratory of Sant Orsola al Consolato in the Piazza del Popolo. Cavalieri Acciajoli and Abate Panciatici attended Guido as confessors, while Abati Marascelli and Honorato Mattei attended his confederates. These were members of the Confraternia della Misericordia – the Brotherhood of Death and Pity, founded in 1488 – whose duty it was to prepare condemned prisoners for execution. Like all the brothers of their order, they wore forbidding black cassocks and pointed hoods, their eyes sunken and unseen behind the slits cut for them.

Guido behaved well from the first, his only request being that he should not be publicly executed. But that, he was told, was inevitable, and he must reconcile himself to it. His only response was: 'And must I die in this way because I defended and maintained my honour?' He made a full confession, then knelt for a quarter of an hour before the altar. The others were also confessed – Baldeschi admitted to several other murders done before he took up with Guido; he had once killed four travellers after robbing them. Only Agostinelli refused to confess or repent. He was innocent, he said; nobody had ever told him anything about the murderous plot; he had simply been instructed to guard the door and let nobody in. Two more senior priests were sent for – Abate Vannini, Canon of St Peter's, and Abate Maggi, Canon of the Lateran Basilica. They were no more successful at first, but after some time Agostinelli said he would confess –

but on condition they granted him a favour. While in prison, he had been befriended by an older prisoner, who had been sentenced to the galleys for a trivial offence. If this man's sentence were commuted to banishment, he would make his peace with God.

His confessors, eager that his soul should be saved, went away and came back with the other prisoner's rosary, which Agostinelli recognised. That would not do, he said; he must see the man himself. The other prisoner was sent for, brought to the chapel, and assured that he would be released. When he had left, however, Agostinelli remained obdurate in protesting his innocence. The confessors sent for the executioner. He came into the cell, took Agostinelli by the hair, jerked his head back and placed a noose around it. Fear did its work. The man prostrated himself.

Meanwhile, a number of other people had been admitted to the prison, and Guido recognised among them Giambatista Rospigliosi, Duke of Zagarolo and Prince of the Holy Roman Empire. He begged the Duke's pardon if he had seemed preoccupied and failed to greet him with proper respect, and asked for a few minutes' conversation, imploring him to be so good as to keep in touch with his surviving relatives and see that they needed for nothing, and in particular to attempt to discover the whereabouts of Abate Paolo and comfort him. The Duke consented (but, it seems, never attempted to fulfil the charge).

Guido now sat down at a bare table in his cell and dictated his will, leaving money for masses to be said for his soul and the souls of his victims, and ending with the hope that 'if men of this world had been capable of depriving him of his wife's dear company in this life, they would not be able to do so in the next'. He left two *scudi*, found on him when he was arrested – about £42 – to a fellow prisoner.

In the Via Giulia outside the prison five tumbrils were assembled, and at one o'clock Guido and his four accomplices were brought down the stairs from the row of condemned cells on the roof of the Carceri Nuove and placed in them, one in each, arms (some still painful from the dislocating torture of the *strapado*) bound behind their backs. Each man was accompanied by a priest who held a cross steadily before his eyes as the carts set off through streets so crowded that at times the procession was forced to a halt, onlookers pressing to within a few feet of the condemned men. A way was cleared by the chanting, sombre, black-hooded figures of the Confraternia, and the confessors who had spent the last twelve hours at the prison walked before and after the tumbrils.

When an English visitor to Rome saw just such a procession almost a hundred years later nothing had changed:

First of all there was a procession of priests, one of whom carried a crucifix on a pole hung with black; they were followed by a number of people in long gowns which covered them from head to foot, with holes immediately before the face, through which those in this disguise could see everything perfectly, while they could not be recognised by the spectators . . . All of them carried lighted torches, and a few shook tin boxes into which the multitude put money to defray the expense of masses for the soul of the criminal . . . Immediately after them came the malefactor himself, seated in a cart, with a Capucin Friar on each side of him. The hangman, with two assistants, dressed in scarlet jackets, walked by the cart. . . .

From the steps of the prison Guido and the others passed first through the short Alley of the Evil Way to the Via del Pellegrino, its fashionable and expensive jewellers' shops shut and barred – public executions attracted both pickpockets and more ambitious thieves who used the confusion to enter shops and make off with goods.

The sombre procession then turned left into the Via del Governo Veccio, so narrow that progress became even more awkward, and then into the tiny triangular Piazza Pasquino, where the carts stopped and the condemned men were allowed to alight while priests from the Church of the Agonizzanti administered the last rites, as they did for all condemned criminals who passed their door. The five men all behaved courageously.

Guido, on his knees before the church, recited some verses of the *Miserere* so touchingly that many onlookers who were sufficiently close to hear him were reduced to tears. An amateur artist took the opportunity to sketch him, unkempt and miserable, dressed in the clothes he wore when he committed the murder – a brown cloth coat and black shirt and a goats-hair cloak. His neck was bare for the axe, and a shapeless hat was pulled over his head. Agostinelli, the youngest of his accomplices, also impressed the crowd by his apparent piety and the steadfastness of his gaze upon the cross, while Gambassini rebuked some of the onlookers for weeping – 'saying they were bewailing his good, while he was hastening to join the Lord, so that it might be said that God had touched him with a ray of his mercy . . .'

They were thrust into the carts again, and the cortége crossed the south end of the Piazza Navona, near Bernini's famous fountain, at one side of the crowded market of stalls where John Evelyn, half-a-century earlier, had bought souvenirs of his visit to the city. The crowds grew even thicker, men women and children goggling at the condemned men as they were carried on through the Via dei Canestrari and the Piazza Sant'Eustachio, past the ancient Pantheon to the Piazza Colonna, where favoured customers craned from the windows of the hairdresser's shop where Guido had lounged five years earlier before the whole sordid affair began – and at last to the Corso, the attendants beating back the crowds so that the tumbrils could creep past the church in which he had been married, past the street in which his brother had lived, past the end of the long, narrow Via Vittoria where the house in which he had stabbed his wife and her parents to death still stood empty.

Reaching the Piazza del Popolo, the condemned men descended from the carts and were taken into a temporary shelter built in the garden of the nearby monastery of the Reverend Fathers of the Madonna of the People. Guido paused, recognising some acquaintances and exchanging a few words with them. After a short pause the men were led to the scaffold one by one – first Agostinelli, then Gambassini, Pasquini and Baldeschi. They were hanged.

An onlooker described how Agostinelli, the youngest of the five men, 'at the moment the executioner did his work clasped between his breast and his hands the image of that crucifix whereby they had become certain of Divine Pardon' and 'assured the people of his salvation'. The others were equally collected.

Guido at last was left alone. He asked his confessor if it was not time to go, and was told that he would be informed when that time came. There was a short pause in the entertainment while the bodies of the others were examined and their deaths confirmed. Eventually, they came for Guido, who was allowed the perhaps more comfortable option of death by guillotine – a process used for some time in Italy for the execution of nobles; it was to be almost a hundred years before a perfected version of the instrument was to become notorious in France.

> He went forth courageously and entreated all to pray for his soul, and asking pardon for his sins he mounted the scaffold blindfolded from the Consorteria, with the manacles placed on him by the executioner; and said to all the people that they say a *Pater*, an *Ave* and *Salve Regina* to the Blessed Virgin in order that they might help to that degree his soul, adding that he died for honour . . .

He then stepped forward, knelt, and lay with his head beneath the blade of the guillotine.

> The signal was given to the executioner; the cord controlling the *mannaia* was cut and the head was severed; if the executioner had not been ready to take it, it would have fallen from the scaffold; but he took it up and cried several times in a loud voice, 'This is the head of Guido Franceschini!'

It was 5.30 in the afternoon.

The moment was so dramatic that as the crowd reacted a stand gave way and several people were seen almost to fall from their perches on the rooftops. Astonishingly, no one was killed. The bodies remained on the scaffold for an hour, and were then taken away for burial. Before the crowd dispersed, a collection was taken up in order that masses could be said for the repose of the souls of the executed men.

John Moore described what followed an execution when he was in Rome in the later 1700s:

> During the time appointed by the law for the body to hang, all the members of the procession, with the whole apparatus of torches, crucifixes, and Capucins, went into a neighbouring church at the corner of the Strada del Babuino, and remained there while a mass was said for the soul of the deceased; and when that was concluded they returned in procession to the gallows, with a coffin covered with black cloth. Two persons in masks and with black gowns mounted the ladder and cut the rope, while others below, of the same society, received the body and put it carefully into the coffin.

When the five bodies of the Count and his accomplices were taken down they were carried by the members of the Confraternia to the church of San Giovanni Decollato, where Guido was buried before the altar, the bronze crucifix held before him on his last journey placed nearby. His accomplices were shuffled away elsewhere; rank still counted.

Discussion of the case did not cease with the executions. As one commentator put it:

Rome does not remember a case on which there was such general talk as this. Some defended the Comparini, because they had suffered abuse. Others the Franceschini as it was a matter of honour. But, on looking at the matter dispassionately, they were adjudged to be equally guilty except that Pompilia, who was entirely ignorant of the truth, was without blame; for she had consented to the marriage at the command of her mother without the knowledge of her father, and had fled from her husband for fear of death with which he had often unjustly threatened her.

Neither did legal action end with the beheading of Guido, for now there was an argument over Pompilia's property, brought by or on behalf of the Convent of Santa Maria Magdalena. This convent had been founded in 1520 by Pope Leo X for the rehabilitation of 'immoral women', and had become known as the Convent of the Convertites. It was governed by the Archfraternity of Charity, which was entitled to the property of 'fallen women' who either died intestate or had neglected to leave a proportion of their property to the Archfraternity in their will (which was a condition of the aid given them).

After Pompilia's death, the Convertites immediately attempted to claim their rights. She had inherited all Pietro's property under a will which he had made in 1695, after he and his wife had admitted the truth about her parentage. He left everything in the first place to Violante, but 'when she dies I appoint in her stead . . . Francesca Pompilia, wife of Signor Guido Franceschini of Arezzo.' He went out of his way to pay tribute to Pompilia, who he made his heir 'because of her good character and because for a long time, yes, for many years, I looked upon her in good faith as my daughter, and thought that Signora Violante, my wife and myself were her parents', but he made it a condition of her profiting from the will that she 'seek again her own city and stay here in Rome, in which city I hope she will live chastely and honestly, and will lead the life of a good Christian'. If her marriage were dissolved and she wanted to marry again, or if she decided to enter a nunnery, she was to have the use of 1,000 *scudi* (some £21,200) – though he advised her not to marry again, 'lest she subject herself a second time to other deceptions'. He added, on a rather sour note, that if Guido should die before Pompilia, about 700 *scudi* of the dowry the latter had received – about £14,800 – should revert to her, 'which I think would be at least very difficult, if not impossible, because Signor Guido is wretchedly poor and his family is very poor'.

Despite this, the Procurator for the convent continued to argue that Pompilia had led an evil life, and that any property she had left should not pass to her son, Gaetano, but should be theirs under the terms of the convent's foundation. Domenico Tighetti, the executor of the will, contested this argument. The case was heard by the same Lieutenant Governor of Rome, Marco Antonio Venturini, who had presided at the two trials.

The case for not depriving Pompilia's son of her estate was argued by Antonio Lamparelli. He first made it clear that he had been careful not to open his case before the end of the prosecution of Guido lest he might prejudice the trial – he had, after all, defended Pompilia at the Prosecution for Elopement. Now that the matter had been brought to an end and the executions had taken place, however, he wished to argue that 'the memory of the aforesaid Pompilia should be absolutely freed from the crime of adultery injustly and too bitterly fastened upon her by her husband, and that it should be declared by a definitive decree that she has not violated her marriage vow.'

The story was gone over yet again, the same facts and inventions recited, the same letters read and argued over, though less comprehensively – they were, after all, fresh in the judge's mind. On 19 August 1698 Venturini pronounced in favour of Tighetti:

> *Proof is not established as regards the pretended adultery*, and therefore the memory of the same Francesca Pompilia should be and is *entirely* restored to her pristine good name and reputation.

# White Shall Not Neutralise the Black

> White shall not neutralise the black, nor good
> Compensate bad in man, absolve him so:
> Life's business being just the terrible choice.

And there the case rests. Unless new documents surface in some Italian library, we know all we are likely to know about the Franceschini and Comparini families, and the tragedy of 1698. There is much more we would wish to know. What happened to Gaetano, Pompilia's child? He vanishes from history as though he had never been. We have no description of him, no idea what he looked like or how he behaved, no idea whether he was brought up by Tighetti, placed in an orphanage, adopted by friends . . . As far as we can guess, Tighetti seems to have been a considerate and kindly man (although we should remember that he probably stood to gain financially from getting control of Pompilia's small fortune), so we can only hope that the little boy grew up into a life more fortunate than that of either his mother or her husband. As for his probable father, Caponsacchi – it would be too much to hope that that young man returned out of the blue to claim such an encumbrance as a motherless child. He eventually went back to Arezzo, resigned as Canon of the Pieve, and is heard of no more, though his family was still living in the town until 1775 – as were the Guillichini.

Little remains to tell of the other characters. Beatrice Franceschini died in 1701 in Arezzo. News of Abate Paolo came home to Rome in 1699 from Prague where a poem was published carrying his name; in 1708 he turned up in Milan, and was in the train of the Duca de Moles on a visit to Barcelona. The whole family then seemed to die out; at least there is no record of their being in Arezzo after Beatrice's death, and the house in which the family lived has at some time been demolished.

The characters of this Roman murder story are only dimly seen in the cool and largely unemotional reports of the various lawsuits and trials that have come down to us. Very occasionally we glimpse their physical presence through someone else's eyes – when Guido was sketched on his way to his execution, or when Pompilia's aunt recalls recognising the infant as her niece 'because she had my sister's nose, and I should recognise her by her eyes, because they were large . . .' The personalities of the main protagonists, however, come strongly through even the bald reporting of the trial and the circumstances surrounding it.

Guido Franceschini was clearly not a handsome man. Although no one is likely to look his best on his way to be executed, the rough sketch we have (see plates between pages 146 and 147) seems accurate enough. He was seriously hampered, too, by lack of charm and lack of intelligence. Though appointed a sub-deacon, he seems (unlike three of his brothers) not to have been at all interested in the Church, which may be one of the reasons why his appointment under Cardinal Nervi did not last long; he lacked the intelligence and application to find another position. This in itself must have been aggravating – his brother Paolo had a successful career in Church service in Rome, while Guido was reduced to looking about for a wealthy bride. It was not a circumstance likely to sweeten the character. A younger brother who has repudiated his inheritance is no great catch, and he was fortunate to come across the Comparini, as eager to make an advantageous match for their daughter as he was to marry well. That his bride's family were not very high on the social scale was neither here nor there – he had enough noble blood for them both, and was extremely proud of it. Indeed his pride in his noble ancestry was one of the mainsprings of his life. Money was another; the need for a child the third.

Guido was careful with what money he had, and possibly pleased at first that Pietro Comparini was almost equally careful – the two men were at one in deciding that all the legal work on the dowry should be done in Rome, where lawyers were cheaper than they were in Arezzo. He was also jealous of his reputation: Pietro's taste for low company was one of the most irritating aspects of the families' uneasy relationship in Arezzo. Such a man was not likely to view either the revelations of his wife's illegitimacy or her elopement with equanimity. If he could safely have killed her and Giuseppe Caponsacchi at Castelnuovo when he found them together, he might have done so; Giuseppe's youth, reputation and preparedness probably saved Pompilia and himself at that moment, though Guido was not perhaps so much a coward as a man who found it difficult to take action of any kind. We will never know how strongly his chief associate, Baldeschi, pushed him into action after he heard the news of the birth of Pompilia's child. He may after all have needed very little pushing: clearly, he believed that the boy was Caponsacchi's. His rage, barely under control since Castelnuovo, now took hold, with fatal consequences.

Giuseppe is a more shadowy figure than Guido. We glimpse his fondness for showy clothes as he saunters through the streets of Arezzo, short-sword at his side; we can guess from the exchange of letters between him and Pompilia that he was flattered by her attentions, pleased to be the object of admiration by the beautiful and apparently ill-treated young bride. If he has been presented in these pages as rather the popinjay, that does seem a justifiable view. His relative readiness to help Pompilia escape from her husband is unsurprising, though whether the elopement was truly an elopement remains doubtful. She may have regarded it as such; he, perhaps, as just an amorous adventure, for it seems highly doubtful that he loved her. Had he done so, would he have allowed his sentence of banishment to prevent him from coming to her when their son was born? If, indeed, the child was their son. It seems likely that he was; there is more than enough circumstantial evidence to suggest that they slept together in Guido's bed at Arezzo before the 'elopement' was ever thought of. All in all, Giuseppe Caponsacchi does not come out of the story particularly well.

But who does? Abate Paolo, perhaps. Browning made him a villain, but in fact he did all he could from the beginning to mend fences between the two families, treating the Franceschini with a degree of respect which they certainly did not deserve. Pietro and Violante were out for themselves from the beginning. The best thing that can be said of Pietro is that he loved his adopted daughter – even after learning the truth about her birth, he spoke kindly of her, never for a moment thought of rejecting her, spoke well of her in his Will. There seem to be no positive tributes one can pay to Violante, who from the very beginning was out for money, who betrayed and lied, and who certainly did nothing to make life any easier at Arezzo by treating the nobly born Beatrice Franceschini with contempt.

And what of Pompilia? Saint or sinner? Certainly not the former, though Browning saw and presented her as such. His contemporaries, with one or two exceptions, accepted his portrayal. But there was always room for doubt about her character and morality. She did, after all, take some of her husband's money together with the clothes and jewellery she packed when she left Arezzo – and also some clothes of her husband's; this may have been no more than spite, a venial sin. But the Tuscan judges condemned her for theft as well as adultery. At the trial for elopement, Giuseppe's lawyer's claim that he needed to spend the night in her room in order to protect her struck a dumb note; it sounds more like an excuse for spending the night together, and a needless excuse at that, for everyone knew that shared rooms were the rule rather than the exception. The Cortona Codex revealed a document in which Guido's lawyers pointed out the contradictions between the statements made by the two accused both about the time of arrival at Castelnuovo and exactly what happened there. It may be that the couple did not sleep together at Castelnuovo – or, rather, that they did nothing more. So long a journey over dreadful roads in a rickety carriage can scarcely be regarded as aphrodisiac, and even two young and virile lovers might well have been too exhausted at the end of it to do anything but fall into unconsciousness.

Whatever the truth might be about that night, we may suspect that Pompilia had already started a relationship with Giuseppe before their flight, for though it was claimed that she was so closely watched that she would have had no opportunity for adultery, she herself admitted to at least two occasions when she was alone with Giuseppe in Guido's absence. In one of her letters she advised Giuseppe to use a side-door when the street-door was locked, and both she and Giuseppe referred to her maid Maria as a go-between. The evidence of a neighbour was dismissed because she was alleged to be a prostitute. The evidence of prostitutes has similarly been discounted in our own time, presumably on the grounds that a woman who will sell herself will also sell the truth. But there is no real reason to doubt that Maria Margherita Contenti was telling the truth when she said she saw Pompilia letting Giuseppe out of the house.

Were the letters produced, allegedly exchanged between Pompilia and Giuseppe, genuine? The prosecution said that they were forgeries, and Pompilia claimed that she had either never written them, or that some had been traced by her over pencilled originals written by Guido. Surely this cannot be the case. Such botched documents would have told their own story, and the fact that her lawyers failed to produce experts to support her story must convince us that she in fact wrote the letters. His protest that he had not written those he sent her in reply sounds hysterical, and the lawyers at the trial for elopement were as unwilling as Pompilia's to put them to the test.

It was always possible, even likely, that Pompilia was Giuseppe Caponsacchi's mistress, and that her child was his. Though she may well have been a month pregnant when she left Arezzo, she concealed her state from Guido despite his eagerness for a child. The Comparini seem to have been eager to conceal her state from him, too, until the birth had taken place, and even then the baby was sent out of their house the moment it was born.

Much has been made of her death-bed assertions of innocence; but apart from any doubts about whether she might have lied to her priests, it has been pointed out that after making her confession, she was technically innocent, and may have felt free to assert the fact. Her confessors, realising that the defence would make much of the pretended fact that Caponsacchi was 'a priest', would have been eager to defend his innocence as well as hers. A number of the priests who were at her death-bed were beneficiaries under her will, and would have lost their legacies had she been declared guilty of adultery. In an interesting article on the case, Professor P.E. Beichner asserts that no confessor is likely to testify to a court of law about a penitent unless he is under some kind of pressure, and because he must not reveal what he hears in confession, he is likely to give a favourable impression just because silence would seem to be an admission of the penitent's guilt. 'In an ecclesiastical court,' he writes, 'such testimony of a confessor would be worthless, and volunteered testimony of anyone else would be suspect.'

So there the matter rests. The mystery that remains is only the mystery attached to extreme acts arising from extreme emotions. If Browning saw the story in black and white, we can now see it in its original grey, with perhaps not a great deal to choose between the Franceschini and the Comparini as to virtue, and with Pompilia caught between the two families, the pitiful heroine of what remains one of the most fascinating murder stories of the early seventeenth century.

# Robert Browning's The Ring and the Book

*Here it is, this I toss and take again;*
*Small-quarto size, part print part manuscript:*
*A book in shape but, really, pure crude fact*
*Secreted from man's life when hearts beat hard,*
*And brains, high-blooded, ticked two centuries since . . .*

Robert Browning was convinced of Pompilia's innocence from the beginning, and she became in his mind more and more saintly as time went on. He spent four years actually writing *The Ring and the Book*. At first he worked in rhymed couplets, but he found the rhymes too difficult to sustain and turned to blank verse. He continued to research, asking the painter Frederick Leighton, for instance, kindly to go to the church of San Lorenzo in Lucina and describe its interior. He wrote for three hours each morning, starting at five o'clock whether he was in Florence or in London – even when travelling. There was no time for play: 'The business of getting done with some twenty thousand lines very effectually suppressed any impulse to whistle between-whiles!' he commented.

He was determined to make a great work of art not only as a proof of his powers as a poet, but as a memorial to his wife. The lines flowed remarkably swiftly from his pen: 8,400 had been completed by July 1865, rising to 15,000 in May of the following year, and to over 20,000 by July 1867.

He decided to tell the story from the point of view of a number of characters: particularly, of course, Guido, Pompilia and Giuseppe, but also two of the lawyers, Arcangeli and Bottini, and the Pope, to whom he gives the final word. Then he thickened the texture by giving the point of view of the people in Rome who so busily and animatedly discussed the case in their drawing-rooms and bars – 'Half-Rome', 'The Other Half-Rome', and 'Tertium Quid'. Much of the material for these three sections came from the two anonymous accounts of the trial and the events leading up to it which were tipped into the leaves of *The Old Yellow Book*. A Preface and an Afterword completed the book. The first volume was issued in December 1868; the following three in the spring of 1869. There was a second edition within six months. Browning was confident that he had produced something good, something lasting, something subtle. He told his friend William Allingham frankly, 'It's admirable! A builder will tell you sometimes of a house, "there's twice as much work underground as above", and so it is with my poem.'

The critical reception supported him – it was almost unanimously enthusiastic. The *Athenæum*, the *Fortnightly*, the *Edinburgh Magazine*, the *London Quarterly*, the *Revue des Deux Mondes* – all the most important periodicals – were unanimous in praise of the poem. Robert Buchanan, the critic of the *Athenæum*, wrote: 'We must record at once our conviction, not merely that *The Ring and the Book* is beyond all parallel the supremest poetical achievement of our time, but that it is the most precious and profound spiritual treasure that England has produced since the days of Shakespeare', while the *Edinburgh Review* remarked that 'In English literature the creative faculty of the poet has not produced three characters more beautiful or better to contemplate than [the Pope, Caponsacchi and Pompilia].' Walter Baghot (in *Tinsley's Magazine*) said of the first published section that Browning 'had never written anything more powerful than the tragic story which is there conceived and developed'.

Henry James might well have made something of the story – his prose is not unlike Browning's poetry, after all, in its particular difficulty, and he certainly approached his novels much as the poet approached his narrative poems. James thought seriously about how he might have tackled the story of Guido and Pompilia, for in 1912 he gave a lecture on Browning's poem at Caxton Hall in London, which he entitled 'The Novel in *The Ring and the Book*', showing how it might have been written as prose fiction. He spoke of the Rome of the period as a wonderful setting for a story: '. . . Italy of the eve of the eighteenth century – a vast painted and gilded rococo shell roofing over a scenic, an amazingly figured and furnished earth but shutting out almost the whole of our own dearly-bought rudely-recovered spiritual sky'. And what a story! – it cried out for prose; there was not a detail of Pompilia's elopement over the Apennines – 'the long hours when they melt together only *not* to meet – that doesn't positively plead for our perfect prose transcript'. But he nevertheless praised Browning's poem, and the particular quality in it which interested him: 'the great constringent relation between man and woman at once its maximum and as the relation most worth while in life for either party'.

There were, of course, those that did not think *The Ring and the Book* so fine as all that. Browning himself had some doubts about its reception by readers for whom the subject itself might seem too earthy:

> Well, British Public, ye who like me not,
> (God love you!) and will have your proper laugh
> At the dark question, laugh it! I laugh first.

And indeed, one or two critics disliked its realism. J.H.C. Fane, in the *Edinburgh Review*, thought that

Browning 'ventures with Pompilia upon ground of perilous lubricity . . . There is both lapse and collapse of all that preserves the self-respect of art in the occasional outrages of thought and language – in one instance, the mental and verbal garbage – which he assigns to male characters in the drama.' Others shared his view, but all agreed with the anonymous reviewer in *Chamber's Journal* that while 'for the choice of subject we have nothing but condemnation . . . there is no mark of great and noble poetry wanting in the elaboration of this noble masterpiece.'

Some friends had their reservations. Edward Fitzgerald, the translator of *The Rubáiyát of Omar Khayyám*, failed to finish the poem: 'I have been trying in vain to read it . . . but then, I never could read Browning', while Thomas Carlyle, though he thought the Italian atmosphere and characterisation excellent, told Allingham that he thought the whole thing was 'on a most absurd basis. The real story is plain enough on looking into it; the girl and the handsome young priest were lovers.' Allingham himself had his doubts about the work: he remarked to Carlyle – and even to Browning himself – that he thought the poet 'had neither given us the real story as he found it, nor, on the other hand, constructed a poem out of it, and in reading *The Ring and the Book* I felt . . . like a creature with one leg and one wing, half hopping, half flying . . .' But the publisher of the work turned out to have a good eye for poetry. While Browning had never previously commanded a wide popular readership, the public took to *The Ring and the Book*, and the four volumes sold well – so well that he was offered £1,250 for the right of publication for five years, and a third edition came out in 1869.

*The Ring and the Book* marked the beginning of Browning's real popularity with the public. Previously, his work had been caviare to the general – his poems were considered 'difficult'. Tennyson, after tackling the earlier narrative poem 'Sordello', remarked abrasively: 'There were only two lines in it that I understood, and they were both lies: "Who will may hear Sordello's story told" and "Who would has heard Sordello's story told"', while Carlyle reported that his wife had 'read through "Sordello" without being able to make out whether "Sordello" was a man, or a city, or a book.' His ambitious new work changed the popular view. As his friend Alexandra Orr wrote, 'henceforth whatever he published was sure of ready acceptance, of just, if not always enthusiastic, appreciation' – and she shrewdly went on to make the very first public association of Pompilia with Elizabeth Barrett Browning:

We cannot read the emotional passages of *The Ring and the Book* without hearing in it a voice which is not Mr Browning's own: an echo, not of his past, but from it. The remembrance of that past must have accompanied him through every stage of the great work. Its subject had come to him in the last days of his greatest happiness. It had lived with him, though in the background of consciousness, through those of his keenest sorrow. It was his refuge in that aftertime, in which a subsiding grief often leaves a deeper sense of isolation. He knew the joy with which his wife would have witnessed the diligent performance of this his self-imposed task. The beautiful dedication contained in the first and last books was only a matter of course. But Mrs Browning's spiritual presence on this occasion was more than a presiding memory of the heart. I am convinced that it entered largely into the conception of Pompilia, and, so far as this depended on it, the character of the whole work.

Browning himself obviously felt deeply about his heroine. The critic of art and literature Professor Sir Sidney Colvin remembered his reading of the Pompilia section of the poem 'in which he could control neither his voice nor his tears, and had nearly all his audience in tears with him'.

*The Ring and the Book* made Browning one of the two most popular poets of his time. Luck was a factor – luck and timing, which was nothing to do with poetry. English readers had just discovered the delights of reading about 'great trials'. As Leslie Stephen pointed out, reading accounts of trials 'we assist at a series of tragedies which may shock our sense of justice, but in their rough-and-ready fashion go at once to the point and show us all the passions of human beings fighting in deadly earnest over the issues of life and death'. That is certainly true of the story told in *The Old Yellow Book*.

The poem opens with a general introduction during which Browning describes how he found *The Old Yellow Book*, a summary of how he intends to present it in verse, and finally the moving dedication to his late wife:

> O lyric Love, half-angel and half-bird
> And all a wonder and a wild desire, –
> Boldest of hearts that ever braved the sun . . .

The next three books – 'Half-Rome', 'Other Half-Rome' and 'Tertium Quid' – present three different views of the crime and the trial. First, the story is told by a jealous young man who fears for the virtue of his attractive wife. He has just come from the church where the murdered bodies lie, and takes Guido's side. Wives should be kept in their place, if necessary by whipping:

> Sir, what's the good of law
> In a case o' the kind? None, as she all but says.
> Call in law when a neighbour breaks your fence,
> Cribs from your field, tampers with rent or lease,
> Touches the purse or pocket, – but woos your wife?
> No: take the old way trod when men were men! . . .

> The thing is put right, in the old place, – ay,
> The rod hangs on its nail behind the door,
> Fresh from the brine . . .

In 'The Other Half-Rome', a man speaks who has managed to gain access to Pompilia's house where she lies dying (though Browning sets the scene in a hospital room), and he describes the death-bed. He takes Pompilia's side, presenting the story from her point of view:

> "Earth was made hell to me who did no harm:
> I only could emerge one way from hell
> By catching at the one hand held me, so
> I caught at it and thereby stepped to heaven:
> If that be wrong, do with me what you will!"

'Tertium Quid' is a coxcomb who moves in fashionable circles, and the characters of the tragic event about which he gossips are socially far beneath him. He is out simply to make 'a good story' of the incident – though his sympathies are with Guido, who is at least a 'man of quality' like himself – and, like himself, keen on money and position. Browning has already made the point in Book I:

> Quality took the decent part, of course;
> Held by the husband, who was noble too . . .

But Tertium Quid emphasises the point by describing Pietro and Violante as 'two ghastly scullions' and Pompilia as 'never a pheasant but a carrion-crow.'

With Book V, 'Count Guido Franceschini', Browning begins the serious characterisation of the chief protagonists in the story. He portrays him as addressing the court immediately after having faced the torture of the *strapado*, his arms still aching from the dislocating ropes, ironically refusing the suggestion that he might care to sit:

> Thanks, Sir, but, should it please the reverend Court,
> I feel I can stand somehow, half sit down
> Without help, make shift to even speak, you see,
> Fortified by the sip of . . . why, 'tis wine,
> Velletri, – and not vinegar and gall . . .
> Noblemen were exempt, the vulgar thought,
> From racking, but, since law thinks otherwise,
> I have been put to the rack: all's over now,
> And neither wrist – what men style, out of joint:
> If any harm be, 'tis the shoulder-blade,
> The left one, that seems wrong i' the socket . . .

Guido's defence is – as at the trial – entirely based on the plea that his affronted honour must be satisfied and the affront avenged. He is never, himself, at fault – sinned against, but definitely not sinning; and his family is similarly saintly. Pompilia is a demon: how could anyone fail to sympathise:

That I, having married the mongrel of a drab,
Am bound to grant that mongrel-brat, my wife,
Her mother's birthright-license is as just, –
Let her sleep undisturbed, i'the family style,
Her sleep out in the embraces of a priest,
Nor disallow their bastard as my heir!

Browning pours on the irony, at the same time making it clear that he sees Guido as a devil – satanic but human. The Count makes his excuses on cold, calculated grounds, while appealing at the same time to the emotions – he is a nobleman, of the same class as the judge. He skilfully uses the cards of flattery and false humility, and ends with a plea for the custody of his son, and an openly emotional appeal to the judge's heart, looking towards the Rome that would be if all men were as devoted to the conception of personal honour as he himself:

. . . rife with honest women and strong men,
Manners reformed, old habits back once more,
Customs that recognise the standard worth, –
The wholesome household rule in force again,
Husbands once more God's representatives,
Wives like the typical Spouse once more . . .

Browning was good at villains – look at the masterly oblique portrait of the narrator of 'My Last Duchess';

but Guido is his masterpiece in the genre. Greed, self-importance and misanthropy are at his dark heart. The depth of his degeneracy is shown again, even more forcefully, in Book XI, set in the condemned cell during the last minutes before the Count is led down to the waiting tumbrils. The two confessors, Cardinal Acciajoli and Abate Panciatici, are with him and listen to his wild speech as his reason almost gives way. He still justifies his actions, on behalf of all married men:

> All honest Rome approved my part;
> Whoever owned wife, sister, daughter, – nay,
> Mistress, – had any shadow of any right
> That looks like right, and, all the more resolved,
> Held it with tooth and nail, – these manly men
> Approved!

He rails against all those who have condemned him in a masterpiece of self-justification such as Iago might have uttered had he not sworn to hold his tongue, rails at Pompilia ('a little saucy rose-red minx'), at the public, the court, his lawyers:

> And then my Trial, – 'tis my Trial that bites
> Like a corrosive, so the cards are packed,
> Dice loaded, and my life-stake tricked away!
> Look at my lawyers, lacked they grace of law,
> Latin or logic? Were they not fools to the height,

Fools to the depth, fools to the level between,
O' the foolishness set to decide the case?
They feign, they flatter; nowise does it skill,
Everything goes against me . . .

Finally his mind gives way in terror as he hears outside his cell the tramp of the feet of the men coming to escort him to his execution:

Life is all!
I was just stark mad, – let the madman live
Pressed by as many chains as you please pile!
Don't open! Hold me from them! I am yours,
I am the Granduke's – no, I am the Pope's!
Abate, – Cardinal, – Christ, – Maria, – God, . . .
Pompilia, will you let them murder me?

It is a magnificent *tour de force*.

In Book VI Giuseppe Caponsacchi steps forward. His narrative too is highly emotional – he knows that as he speaks, Pompilia lies dying. Browning follows the example of the prosecution at Guido's trial, and makes Giuseppe a priest; this gives him the opportunity to contrast his Biblical allusions and parallels with the blasphemous allusions of Guido, who in his monologue portrays himself, ludicrously, as almost a Christ-like figure. Giuseppe sees himself rather as St George – a representative of the Church as defender of the innocent – but hanging between temptation and commitment. He is not an innocent: half-Rome reports that he was known at 'a certain haunt of doubtful fame,' and the Pope speaks of him visiting a 'wanton'. But now, with Pompilia lying on her death-bed, he feels he has been redeemed by her, having learned:

> To have to do with nothing but the true
> The good, the eternal – and these, not alone
> In the main current of the general life,
> But small experiences of every day,
> Concerns of the particular hearth and home:
> To learn not only by a comet's rush
> But a rose's birth, – not by the grandeur, God –
> But the comfort, Christ.

Browning portrays a priest who is also a decent young man whose honourable conduct is equal to that of Pompilia, and who is certainly guiltless of the slightest familiarity with her: at Castelnuovo:

> I never touched her with my finger-tip
> Except to carry her to the couch, that eve,
> Against my heart, beneath my head, bowed low,
> As we priests carry the paten . . .

He is not without spirit: faced with Guido at the inn and taunted by him,

> I stood as near
> The throat of him – with these two hands, my own, –
> As now I stand near yours, Sir, – one quick spring,
> One great good satisfying gripe, and lo!
> There had he lain abolished with his lie,
> Creation purged o'the miscreate, man redeemed,
> A spittle wiped off from the face of God!

Then he tells the court how Guido led the officers up the stone steps to the room in which Pompilia lay:

> Composed as when I laid her, that last eve,
> O'the couch, still breathless, motionless, sleep's self,
> Wax-white, seraphic, saturate with the sun
> O'the morning that now flooded from the front
> And filled the window with a light like blood.
> 'Behold the poisoner, the adulteress,
> – And feigning sleep too! Seize, bind!' – Guido hissed.

Next, at the very centre of the poem, Browning turns in Book VII to his heroine, Pompilia, who he sees rather as she was seen on her death-bed, by her confessor: not only as a human being, but as saint and martyr. In his portrait of her he sets out his concept of ideal womanhood – as Eve, as Madonna, as rose, as dove, as sacrificial lamb.

Browning sketches her first in Book VI, where Giuseppe describes her face:

Her brow had not the right line, leaned too much,
Painters would say; they like the straight-up Greek:
This seemed bent somewhat with an invisible crown
Of martyr and saint, not such as art approves.
And how the dark orbs dwelt deep underneath,
Looked out of such a sad sweet heaven on me –
The lips, compressed a little, came forward too,
Careful for a whole world of sin and pain.

Now he allows her to tell her own story, in over 1,800
lines of verse, to her confessor, Fra Celestino, and the
others gathered about her death-bed.

I am just seventeen years and five months old,
And, if I lived one day more, three full weeks;
'Tis writ so in the church's register,
Lorenzo in Lucina, all my names
At length, so many names for one poor child,
– Francesca Camilla Vittoria Angela
Pompilia Comparini, – laughable!
Also 'tis writ that I was married there
Four years ago; and they will add, I hope,
When they insert my death, a word or two . . .
This, in its place, this which one cares to know,
That I had been a mother of a son
Exactly two weeks . . .

The tone of her Book is so saintly that one might think it would cloy; in contrast to Giuseppe, she is all forbearance, piety, restraint, resignation – if he is the church militant, she is the church submissive. Browning brings off a remarkable image of goodness (so much more difficult to characterise than evil). He does not allow Pompilia to plead for pity or take the attitude of a martyr – simply to convey the disappointment of a young girl who had hoped for a husband very different to

> Guido Franceschini, – old
> And nothing like so tall as I myself,
> Hook-nosed and yellow in a bush of beard,
> Much like a thing I saw on a boy's wrist,
> He called an owl and used for catching birds . . .

She had hoped, too, for a marriage very different than the one in which she found herself:

> – just such a surprise,
> Such a mistake, in that relationship!
> Everyone says that husbands love their wives,
> Guard them and guide them, give them happiness;
> 'Tis duty, law, pleasure, religion: well,
> You see how much of this comes true in mine!
> People indeed would fain have somehow proved
> He was no husband: but he did not hear,
> Or would not wait, and so has killed us all.

Then there is . . . only let me name one more!
There is the friend, – men will not ask about,
But tell untruths of, and give nicknames to,
And think my lover, most surprise of all!
Do only hear, it is the priest they mean,
Giuseppe Caponsacchi: a priest – love,
And love me! Well, yet people think he did.

She tells her story movingly, if resignedly; but there are moments of joy – as in the passage in which she remembers the morning on which she rose from bed determined to leave Arezzo and her husband:

    Up I sprang alive,
Light in me, light without me, everywhere
Change! A broad yellow sun-beam was let fall
From heaven to earth, – a sudden drawbridge lay,
Along which marched a myriad merry motes,
Mocking the flies that crossed them and recrossed
In rival dance, companions newborn too.
On the house-eaves, a dripping shag of weed
Shook diamonds on each dull grey lattice-square,
As first one, then another bird leapt by,
And light was off, and lo was back again,
Always with one voice, – where are two such joys? –
The blessed building-sparrow! I stepped forth,
Stood on the terrace, – o'er the roofs, such sky!
My heart sang . . .

But such moments are rare: the horror of her marriage is vividly conveyed:

> That night my husband bade
> '–You, whom I loathe, beware you break my sleep
> This whole night! Couch beside me like the corpse
> I would you were!'

As for Giuseppe, he is the 'lover of my life, O soldier-saint'. She had already made quite clear, quoted in Book II, what she owed him:

> 'Earth was made hell to me who did no harm:
> I only could emerge one way from hell
> By catching at the one hand held me, so
> I caught at it and thereby stepped to heaven:
> If that be wrong, do with me what you will!'

In her own narrative Pompilia pays additional tribute to Giuseppe:

> And this man, men call sinner? Jesus Christ!
> Of whom men said, with mouths Thyself mad'st once
> 'He hath a devil' – say he was Thy saint,
> My Caponsacchi!

And calls on him with her dying breath:

Tell him, — I know not wherefore the true word
Should fade and fall unuttered at the last —
It was the name of him I sprang to meet
When came the knock, the summons and the end.

In Books VIII and IX Browning turns to two of the lawyers, Arcangeli and Bottini. These are perhaps the weakest sections of the poem, and Browning makes no attempt to be faithful to what is known of the lawyers' characters. Indeed, he caricatures them. Arcangeli is shown playing with his eight-year-old son while trying to get the papers for the case in order; but he seems less worried about the case than the success of the little boy's birthday party, and indeed the success of the meal he has planned, with the

Minced herb
That mollifies the liver's leathery slice,
With here a goose-foot, there a cock's-comb stuck,
Cemented in an element of cheese.

It is understandable that Browning felt a little light relief should interrupt the intense drama of the poem; but his humour is not always successful, and the book slows almost to a halt as Arcangeli translates, word by word and line by line, the legal Latin of *The Old Yellow Book*:

> *Mulier Smirnea quœdam*, good my lords,
> A gentlewoman lived in Smyrna once,
> *Virum et filium ex eo conceptum*, who
> Both husband and her son begot by him,
> Killed, *interfecerat, ex quo*, because,
> *Vir filium suum perdiderat*, her spouse
> Had been beforehand with her, killed her son
> *Matrimonii primi*, of a previous bed.

Bottini, in Book IX, is depicted as a pompous and self-regarding showman, rehearsing to himself the ornate speeches he will make in court, which focus strongly on Pompilia's supposed lustfulness and dishonesty. He is in the law simply for the income and public regard his practice brings him, and is very happy indeed to be Bottini the Advocate, impressing the court with his interminable prose, impatient when told to shorten his speeches, but happy to take the money:

> There's my oration – much exceeds in length
> That famed Panegyric of Isocrates,
> They say it took him fifteen years to pen.
> But all those ancients could say anything!
> He put in just what rushed into his head,
> While I shall have to prune and pare and print.
> This comes of being born in modern times
> With priests for auditory. Still, it pays.

In a sense, the eighth and ninth books echo the second and third, putting contrary arguments just as the Roman people put their opposing points of view. Browning took considerable dramatic licence with his two characters: there is nothing in their reported speeches to the court to support his characterisation of them; but in dramatic poems, as in lapidary inscriptions (to quote Dr Johnson) a man is not on oath.

The tenth book of the poem, in which the Pope considers the appeal of the condemned men, was the most admired section of the work when it was published: 'a fitting organ-peal to close such a book of mighty music', as one reviewer put it. It remains arguably the most impressive.

The 86-year-old Pope (in fact, Innocent XII was 83) sits alone, having considered the case and already decided that Guido and his confederates must die, but thinking of the power of life and death which has been put into his hands, and turning for solace to a book of the lives of previous Popes:

> I have the Papacy complete
> From Peter first to Alexander last;
> Can question each and take instruction so.

He clearly does not consider himself to be infallible, and finds it impossible to believe Pompilia and Giuseppe entirely innocent, or indeed to decide the true extent of Guido's guilt – though guilty he clearly is. As a modern commentary puts it, the Pope sees the Roman murder case as Browning wishes us to see it – as a kind of morality play, with characters representing the forces of good and evil, truth and error, in conflict; and with implications far exceeding the mere guilt, innocence or fate of several individual human beings.

The Pope's monologue is Browning at his best – dramatic, thoughtful, characteristic, forceful, clear in vision and discerning in argument. He sees Guido, for instance, as a fallen man – whose life started advantageously,

> Fortified by propitious circumstance,
> Great birth, good breeding, with the Church
> for guide . . .

But Guido was driven to madness chiefly by the revelation of Pompilia's low birth, and led by his insane fury to persecute her. Pompilia herself the Pope finds guiltless, 'Perfect in whiteness'; Giuseppe, he sees as a 'warrior-priest', almost equally blameless. But for Guido and his companions there can be no mercy. He orders the scaffold to be set up,

> Not in the customary place, by Bridge
> Saint Angelo, where die the common sort;
> But since the man is noble, and his peers

> By predilection haunt the People's Square,
> There let him be beheaded in the midst,
> And his companions hanged on either side . . .

Of course there is still hope for mercy for Guido, from a superior hand. The frail old Pope's last words are worth quoting in full:

> For the main criminal I have no hope
> Except in such a suddenness of fate.
> I stood at Naples once, a night so dark
> I could have scarce conjectured there was earth
> Anywhere, sky or sea or world at all:
> But the night's black was burst through by a blaze –
> Thunderstruck blow on blow, earth groaned and bore,
> Through her whole length of mountain visible:
> There lay the city thick and plain with spires,
> And, like a ghost disshrouded, white the sea.
> So may the truth be flashed out by one blow,
> And Guido see, one instant, and be saved.
> Else I avert my face, nor follow him
> Into that sad obscure sequestered state
> Where God unmakes but to remake the soul
> He else made first in vain; which must not be.
> Enough, for I may die this very night
> And how should I dare die, this man let live?

> Carry this forthwith to the Governor.

The horror of Guido's monologue on the early morning of his execution, which appears in Book XI, has already been mentioned; there remains only the final Book, 'The Book and the Ring', in which Browning describes the executions as they are narrated in a letter from an eye-witness (tipped into his copy of *The Old Yellow Book*) – the early morning confessions, the procession of carts, the scene in the piazza:

> We had the titillation as we sat
> Assembled, (quality in conclave, ha?)
> Of, minute after minute, some report
> How the slow show was winding on its way.
> Now did a car run over, kill a man,
> Just opposite a pork-shop numbered Twelve . . .
> Now did a beggar by Saint Agnes, lame
> From his youth up, recover use of leg
> Through prayer of Guido as he glanced that way:
> So that the crowd near crammed his hat with coin.
> Thus was kept up excitement to the last,
> – Not an abrupt over-bolting, as of yore,
> From Castle, over Bridge and on to block,
> And so all ended ere you well could wink!

He deals with the suit brought by the Convertites, and the final clearing of Pompilia's name, and sums up the case and his book – asking himself why one should try to force or forge Pompilia's story into an artistic framework:

Because it is the glory and good of Art,
That Art remains the one way possible
Of speaking truth, to mouths like mine, at least.
How look a brother in the face and say
'Thy right is wrong, eyes hast thou yet art blind,
Thine ears are stuffed and stopped, despite their length,
And, oh, the foolishness thou countest faith!' . . .

   Art may tell a truth
Obliquely, do the thing shall breed the thought,
Nor wrong the thought, missing the mediate word.
So may you paint your picture, twice show truth,
Beyond mere imagery on the wall, –
So, note by note, bring music from your mind,
Deeper than ever the Andante dived, –
So write a book shall mean, beyond the facts,
Suffice the eye and save the soul beside . . .

# *Notes*

*Page numbers appear in square brackets*

## Abbreviations

RB      Browning, Robert, *The Ring and the Book* (Everyman, J.M. Dent, 1911)

Hodell      *The Old Yellow Book: source of Robert Browning's 'The Ring and the Book'* (tr. and ed. Charles W. Hodell; J.M. Dent, 1911)

Baylor      *Browning's 'Roman Murder Story' as referred to in a hitherto unknown Italian contemporary manuscript* (tr. E.H. Yarrill; Baylor University, Waco, Texas, 1939)

Cortona      The Cortona Codex, as published in *Curious Annals* (ed. Beatrice Corrigan; University of Toronto Press, 1956)

## Introduction

[1]    'Let this old . . .'    RB, I, 824–5.

[4]    'from written title-page . . .'    RB, I, 110–18.

[5]    'a pale, small person . . .'    Hawthorne, Nathaniel, *Italian Notebooks* (London, 1860), pp. 11–13.

[6]    another source . . .    *The death of the wife-murderer Guido Franceschini, by beheading* (Hodell), pp. 259–66.

[7]    'Deplorable and impious homicide . . .'    Cortona, p. xiii.

[8]    Their treatises, often in manuscript . . .    Gest, John Marshall, *The Old Yellow Book* (Philadelphia, 1927).

## Chapter One

[11]    'How very different . . .'    RB, VII, 116–20.

[11]    'as squalid a street . . .'    Silvagni, *Rome, its Princes, Priests and People* (tr. Fanny McLaughlin; London, 1881), p. 98.

[12] 'The streets were without names . . .'   Silvagni, *op. cit.*, p. 121.

[14] in today's money.   In 1700 1 *scudo* was worth 5*s* 5*d* in English currency. The 1700 £ represents £73.96p in the year 2000, so I have worked on the assumption that 1 *scudo* represents £21.20p in contemporary English currency.

[16] Francesca Camilla Vittoria Angela Pompilia . . .   The child, and later the woman, was more often called 'Francesca' than 'Pompilia'. Her nickname, Checca, suggests a childish attempt at the former name. She usually signed herself 'Francesca Pompilia'. I have called her Pompilia throughout because it was under that name that Robert Browning made her famous.

[18] 'broken-spirited and ignorant . . .'   Silvagni, *op. cit.*, p. 76.

[19] no woman could feel safe . . .   Venuti, R., *Descrizione Topografica della Antichita di Roma* (Rome, 1763), p. 27.

[21] In 1681, their father . . .   Cortona, p. xxii.

[24] a list of all his property.   Cortona, p. 9.

[28] 'for their greater quiet . . .'   Cortona, p. 14.

[29] 'every other affectionate regard . . .'   Cortona, p. 16.

[33] 'in an official book . . .'   Cortona, p. 16.

[34] 'peace and love'   Hodell, p. 57.

[36] 'stiff with cold'   Hodell, p. 50.

[39] 'reluctant to engage myself . . .'   Cortona, p. 74.

[40] 'I shudder to think . . .'   Cortona, p. 75.

## Chapter Two

[42] 'Everyone says . . .'   RB, VII, 152–5.

[44] The following afternoon, *et seq*   Cortona, p. 31.

[44] 'I couldn't see . . .'   Cortona, p. 54.

[45] 'When I told Signor Pietro . . .'   Cortona, p. 36.

[45] 'both she and I . . .'   Hodell, p. 161.

[48] 'I told Corona, my mother . . .'   Cortona, p. 47.

[49] 'Francesca Pompilia, wife . . .'   Hodell, p. 161.

[51] 'Dearest Brother-in-law . . .'   Hodell, pp. 56–7.

[53] 'My most Illustrious . . .'   Hodell, pp. 89–90.

[59] 'hussies'   Hodell, p. 91.

[61] Soon she was signing herself . . . All letters quoted are from Hodell, pp. 100–6.

[64] 'I stay in the same room . . .' Hodell, p. 103.

[67] 'the Bishop departs . . .' Hodell, p. 105.

[69] according to the list . . . Hodell, p. 6.

[70] When Goethe . . . Goethe, *Travels in Italy* (London, 1885), p. 284.

[70] the Consular road . . . Anon, *La vera guida per che Viaggia in Italy* (Rome, 1787), p. 97.

[73] 'I am a man . . .' Hodell, p. 246.


## Chapter Three

[74] '. . . a worm must turn . . .' RB, VII, 1592–3.

[74] 'Whoever shall violently assault . . .' Silvagni, *op. cit.*, vol. I, p. 97.

[76] 'My dear father and mother . . .' Hodell, p. 160.

[77] 'The long stone corridors . . .' Treves, Sir Frederick, *The Country of 'The Ring and the Book'* (London, 1913), p. 135.

[78] 'the carrying on and defending . . .' Hodell, p. 162.

[81] found in a latrine. The Cortona Codex states that the letters were found in the latrine of the prison at Castelnuovo where Giuseppe and Pompilia were imprisoned; it seems clear, however, from the *Yellow Book* that the letters were found in the latrine of the inn.

[84] 'I am an honourable man . . .' Cortona, p. 77.

[88] 'complicity in flight . . .' Hodell, p. 106.

[90] 'He said that because of me . . .' Pompilia's statements are paraphrased from the summary of evidence in the *Yellow Book*. No actual witness statements have survived.

[90] '. . . threw some confetti.' Elsewhere the narrative says that sweets were thrown.

[93] 'Cross-questioned about the events . . .' This was a blatant lie – every witness confirmed that the couple had arrived at the inn on the previous evening – a statement the defence was slow to contest.

[95] The Procurator of Charity . . . Hodell, p. 155.

## Chapter Four

[97] 'Vengeance, you know . . .'  RB, II, 1433–6.

[97] 'promises to keep . . .'  Hodell, p. 159.

[98] When he came home . . . Gest, *op cit.*, p. 23.

[102] Unfortunately, in modern times . . .  These arguments were quoted by Giacinto Archangeli in a memorandum to the Governor on behalf of Count Guido during the impending murder trial. Hodell, p. 15.

[104] The spies were clumsy . . .  Baylor, p. 36.

[105] An anonymous writer . . .  Hodell, p. 152.

[107] Not only had the murderers . . .  Cortona, p. 118.

[110] 'so astounded . . .'  Cortona, p. 118.

[110] 'What, is my wife living? . . .'  Hodell, p. 254.

[111] 'During the four days . . .'  Hodell, p. 58.

[113] 'with funereal pomp . . .'  Baylor, p. 41.

## Chapter Five

[114] 'Who is it dares . . .'  RB, II, 1477–8.

[117] as Judge Gest remarks . . .  *op. cit.*, p. 35.

[119] Archangeli got to his feet first . . .  The quotations in this chapter are taken from the reports of the trial in the *Old Yellow Book*, supported on occasion by additional information from the Cortona Codex. The full accounts of the trial as presented in the *Old Yellow Book* are chronologically inexact, very full, repetitious and sometimes muddled. With the help of Judge Gest's corrections (in his *The Old Yellow Book*) and re-translations of some of the passages in Hodell, I have done my best to simplify the reported speeches of the defence and prosecuting lawyers. This has sometimes meant summarising and re-phrasing the original translations.

[131] . . . contradictory statements . . .  None of the statements or alleged confessions have survived.

[132] There were four categories . . .  See Gest, *op. cit.*, pp. 91ff.

[133] In 1556 . . .  Cust, Lionel, *The Cenci* (London, 1929), p. 16.

[134] 'seeming almost to be pleased . . .'  Amidei, Amadeo Barbiellini, *History of Beatrice Cenci* (Rome, 1909), p. 9.

[140] 'the criminal is sewn up . . .'   Gest, *op. cit.*, p. 64.

[140] 'We condemn Giacomo Cenci . . .'   Amidei, *op. cit.*, pp. 29–30.

[143] Nothing is known . . .   Two-hundred-and-twenty years after the execution of the Cenci, the English poet Percy Bysshe Shelley took that case and used it, as Browning did with Pompilia's story, to form the basis for a literary work. He sent the script of *The Cenci* to London in the hope that it could be put on at Covent Garden with the great Charles Kean as Francesco. Alas, though he never actually mentioned incest, the nature of Francesco's crime was obvious and too 'objectionable' for early nineteenth-century audiences. Both Covent Garden and Drury Lane turned it down. It was, however, published – in 1820 – but was only produced for the first time in 1886. Since then the late Sybil Thorndike had a success with it in 1922 and again in 1926, and Barbara Jefford played Beatrice at the Old Vic in 1959.

## Chapter Six

[144] 'A trip . . .'   RB, V, 2056–7.

[145] 'Can you legally flog . . .'   Acts, XXII, 24–6.

[148] 'It is a torture . . .'   De Marsiliis, *De Quaestionibus*, tr. Gest, *op. cit.*, pp. 85–6.

## Chapter Seven

[152] 'Earth was made hell . . .'   RB, III, 1344–7.

[155] So, halfway . . .   Hodell, pp. 145–62.

[162] without any publisher's imprint.   Hodell, pp. 209–26.

## Chapter Eight

[168] 'Sir, what's the good . . .'   RB, II, 1519–24.

[170] Guido's confession . . .   The confessions of Guido and his fellows have not survived; the quotations are from Spreti's summary of them in Hodell.

[170] '. . . they slept together . . .'   These were entirely new and unsupported allegations.

[178] And was it likely . . .   Hodell, p. 104.

[178] Would Pompilia have . . .   Hodell, p. 102.

[184] Dionisio Pignatelli.   Pignatelli's plea was only discovered when the Cortona Codex came to light in 1940. The part he played in the case is obscure, and nothing is known of his history or personality.

## Chapter Nine

[186] 'Pompilia, will you . . .'   RB, XI, 2425.

[186] 'there had been 180 murders . . .'   Collison-Morley, Lacy, *Italy after the Renaissance* (London, 1930), p. 1460.

[186] 'intransigent in his treatment . . .'   Von Pastor, L., *History of the Popes* (ed. F.I. Antrobus; London, 1891), XXXII, pp. 583–6 (quoted Cortona, p. xlvi).

[187] 'He was moved by the fear . . .'   Cortona, p. 92.

[188] Dickens, Charles, *Pictures from Italy* (London, 1845), p. 96.

[189] 'The windows and balconies . . .'   Baylor, p. 45.

[191] The other prisoner . . .   No evidence has been found of his identity, or whether or not he was released.

[192] 'First of all there was a procession . . .'   Moore, John, *A view of Society and Manners in Italy* (London, 1781), p. 154.

[194] 'saying that they were bewailing . . .'   Baylor, p. 44.

[196] 'He went forth courageously. . .'   Baylor, pp. 45–6.

[197] 'During the time . . .'   Moore, *op. cit.*, p. 155.

[198] 'Rome does not remember . . .'   Hodell, pp. 280–1.

[199] 'which I think would be . . .'   Hodell, p. 161.

[200] 'the memory of the aforesaid . . .'   Gest, pp. 563–4.

[200] 'Proof is not established . . .'   Hodell, p. 254.

## Chapter Ten

[201] 'White shall not . . .'   RB, X, 1236–8.

[202] 'because she had my sister's nose . . .'   Cortona, p. 41.

[207] Whatever the truth . . .   Hodell, pp. 101, 103, 104.

[207] she herself admitted . . .   Cortona, xlii.

[208] P.E. Beichner, 'Fra Celestino's Affidavit', *Modern Language Notes*, May 1943, pp. 335–40.

## Epilogue

[210] 'Here it is . . .'   RB I, 84–8.

[212] 'We must record . . .'   *Athenæum*, 20 March 1869, p. 399.

[212] 'In English literature . . .'   *Edinburgh Review*, February 1869, p. 430.

[212] 'had never written anything . . .'   *Tinsley's Magazine*, January 1869, iii.

[213] 'Well, British public . . .'   *The Ring and the Book*, I, 410–12.

[214] 'ventures with Pompilia . . .'   *Edinburgh Review*, July 1869, cxxx.

[214] 'I have been trying in vain . . .'   *Tennyson, a Memoir*, vol. II, p. 59.

[214] 'had neither given us . . .'   Allingham, William, *The Diaries* (London, 1990), p. 186, entry for 2 January 1872.

[215] 'There were only two lines . . .'   Powell, Thomas, *The Living Authors of England* (London), p. 110.

[215] 'We cannot read . . .'   Orr, Mrs Sutherland, *Life and Letters of Robert Browning* (ed. Frederic Kenyon; London, 1908).

[216] 'in which he could control . . .'   Orr, Mrs Sutherland, *op. cit.*, p. 207.

[216] 'we assist at a series of tragedies . . .'   Stephen, Leslie, *Hours in a Library* (London, 1874), vol. III, p. 236.

[217] 'O lyric Love . . .'   RB, I, 1391–3.

[217] 'Sir, what's the good . . .'   RB, II, 1519–24, 1540–2.

[218] "Earth was made hell . . ."   RB, III, 1344–8.

[218] 'Quality took . . .'   RB, I, 276–7.

[219] 'Thanks, Sir . . .'   RB, V, 1–5, 12–17.

[220] 'That I, having married . . .'   RB, V, 88–93.

[220] '. . . rife with honest women . . .'   RB, V, 2039–44.

[221] 'All honest Rome . . .'   RB, XI, 39–44.

[221] 'And then my trial . . .'   RB, XI, 1752–60.

[222] 'Life is all! . . .'   RB, XI, 2419–25.

[223] 'To have to do with nothing . . .'   RB, VI, 2089–96.

[223] 'I never touched her . . .'   RB, VI, 1618–20.

[224] 'I stood as near . . .'   RB, VI, 1473–9.

[224] 'Composed as when I laid her . . .'   RB, VI, 1516–22.

[225] 'Her brow had not . . .'   RB, VI, 1989–96.

[225] 'I am just seventeen . . .'   RB, VII, 1–10, 12–14.

[226] 'Guido Franceschini . . .'   RB, VII, 394–8.

[226] '– just such a surprise . . .'   RB, VII, 150–65.

[227] 'Up I sprang alive . . .'   RB, VII, 1223–37.

[228] 'That night . . .'   RB, VII, 1478–81.

[228] 'Earth was made hell . . .'   RB, III, 1344–8.

[228] 'And this man . . .'   RB, VII, 1483–6.

[229] 'Tell him, – . . .'   RB, VII, 1806–9.

[229] 'Minced herb . . .'   RB, VIII, 117–20.

[230] '*Mulier Smirnea* . . .'   RB, VIII, 912–19.

[230] 'There's my oration . . .'   RB, VIII, 1570–7.

[231] 'I have the Papacy . . .'   RB, X, 10–12.

[232] 'a modern commentary . . .'   Gest, *op. cit.*, p. 69.

[232] 'Fortified by propitious . . .'   RB, X, 478–9.

[232] 'Not in the customary place . . .'   RB, X, 2107–12.

[233] 'For the main criminal . . .'   RB, X, 2116–34.

[234] 'We had the titillation . . .'   RB, XII, 150–5, 159–66.

[235] 'Because it is the glory . . .'   RB, XII, 837–43, 855–63.

# Bibliography

Allingham, William, *Diaries* (Penguin, 1990; entry for 26 May 1868)

Altick Richard D. and, Loucks, James F., *Browning's Roman Murder Story: a reading of 'The Ring and the Book'* (University of Chicago, 1968)

Amidei, Amadeo Barbiellini, *History of Beatrice Cenci* (Rome, 1909)

Anon, *La vera guida per che Viaggia in Italy* (Rome, 1787)

Anon, *The Old Yellow Book: source of Robert Browning's 'The Ring and the Book'* (J.M. Dent, 1911)

Bell, Rudolph M., *How to do it* (University of Chicago, 1999)

Browning, Robert, *The Ring and the Book* (Everyman, J.M. Dent, 1911)

Collison-Morley, Lacy, *Italy after the Renaissance* (G. Routledge & Sons, 1930)

Corrigan, Beatrice (ed.), *Curious Annals* (University of Toronto Press, 1956); 'New Documents on Browning's Roman Murder Case', *Studies in Philology* XLIX (3 July 1952)

Crane, Thomas Frederick, *Italian Social Customs of the Sixteenth Century* (Yale University Press, 1920)

Cust, Sir Lionel, *The Cenci* (Mandrake Press, 1929)

Dickens, Charles, *Pictures from Italy* (London, 1845)

Edel, Lionel, *Henry James: the Master* (London, 1972)

Gest, John Marshall, *The Old Yellow Book* (Philadelphia, 1927)

Goethe, *Travels in Italy* (London, 1885)

Griffin, W. Hall, *The Life of Robert Browning, with notices of his writings, his family and his friends* (Methuen, 1910)

Hawthorne, Nathaniel, *Italian Notebooks* (London, 1860)

Litzinger, Boyd and Smalley, Donald (eds), *Browning: the critical heritage* (Routledge & Kegan Paul, 1970)

Moore, John, *A View of Society and Manners in Italy* (London, 1781)

Orr, Mrs Sutherland, *Life and Letters of Robert Browning* (ed. Frederic Kenyon; London, 1908)

# Bibliography

Peters, Edward, *Torture* (Blackwell, 1985)

Powell, Thomas, *The Living Authors of England* (London, 1851)

Richardson, Joanna, *The Brownings* (Folio Society, 1986)

Silvagni, David, *Rome, its Princes, Priests and People* (tr. Fanny McLaughlin; London 1885, three vols)

Stephen, Leslie, *Hours in a Library* (London, 1874)

Stone, Lawrence, *The Family, Sex and Marriage, 1500–1800* (Weidenfeld & Nicolson, 1977)

Thomas, Donald, *Robert Browning* (Weidenfeld & Nicolson, 1982)

Treves, Sir Frederick, *The Country of 'The Ring and the Book'* (Cassell, 1913)

Venuti, R., *Descrizione Topografica della Antichita di Roma* (Rome, 1763)

Von Pastor, L., *History of the Popes from the Close of the Middle Ages*, vol. XXXII (ed. F.I. Antrobus; London, 1891)

Wise, T.J. (ed.), *Letters of Robert Browning and Elizabeth Barrett* (London, 1973)

Yarril, T.H. (tr.), *Browning's 'Roman Murder Story' as referred to in a hitherto unknown Italian contemporary manuscript* (Baylor University, Waco, Texas, 1939)

# Index

# Index

# *Acknowledgements*

I owe my thanks to the always helpful assistants at the British and London Libraries; to the Librarians of the Italian Cultural Institute, London, and the Library of Balliol College, Oxford; and to Chris Thomas, Chief Information Officer at the Bank of England. I am also grateful for help from Alban McCoy, Dr Eamonn Duffy, Yuri Koszarycz, Senior Lecturer in Religion (Ethics), Australian Catholic University, Frank Mobbs and Isabel Quigley. Lory Reid and Angela Priestman kindly read the manuscript and made a number of helpful suggestions, though responsibility for the text remains, of course, my own. Jaqueline Mitchell and Sarah Moore, my editors, have once more contributed the wisest and most constructive criticism. My wife has, as always, put up with my preoccupation and occasional tetchiness with great good humour, and our dog (with rather less good humour) with postponed and sometimes cancelled walks.

# Nell Gwyn

DEREK PARKER

'lively and entertaining' *The Express*

'[This] lively study paints vivid images both of Nell and of the rollicking self-indulgent goings-on of Charles II's Restoration London.' *Daily Mail*

'. . . a charming volume on an ephemeral, though much-loved figure.' Frank McLynn, *Glasgow Herald*

When Nell Gwyn, an actress on the London stage, first became familiar with the king, she was no better than a prostitute. Yet from the moment Charles II summoned her, there was never any suggestion that she granted her sexual favours to anyone but him; she was as loyal to him as the Queen. On his deathbed Charles prayed neither for his Church nor his people, but asked that 'Nelly might not starve'. Her name is notorious – but what do we really know of this girl who captured the heart of a king? This book reveals the true story of Nell Gwyn against the vivid background of Restoration London.

240PP 198 × 127MM 8PP B/W ILLUSTRATIONS
ISBN 0 7509 2704 6 (PB)

# Who Killed Kit Marlowe?

A Contract to Murder in Elizabethan England

M. J. TROW

Kit Marlowe was the bad boy of Elizabethan drama, a schemer and player who inhabited a seamy underworld in which plots, real and imagined, proliferated. When he died, apparently in a tavern brawl, in Deptford in 1593, stabbed through the eye at the age of 29, it seemed he had only met the death that had been waiting for him. But is this the whole story? Or had Marlowe become embroiled in political intrigue, touched at its edges by the dangers of alchemy, atheism and homosexual love, which made him such a threat to those around him that he had to be expunged? This stylishly written new investigation of Marlowe's death – and the life which provoked it – unravels the evidence to suggest a new answer to a murder which has puzzled us for over four centuries.

M. J. TROW is a crime novelist, biographer and historian. His books include the well-known Lestrade and Maxwell series, and *Let Him Have it Chris – the Murder of Derek Bentley*, which reached *The Times* 100 Bestseller List. He lives in the Isle of Wight.

288PP 234 × 156MM 8PP B/W ILLUSTRATIONS
ISBN 0 7509 2689 9 (HB)

Sutton Publishing is Britain's largest specialist history publisher. Books range from reference to popular biography, the history of ideas, military history, local history, social and cultural history, and heritage; authors from established world experts to first-time writers, and investigative journalists. For further information see the website: **www.suttonpublishing.co.uk**.

We welcome comments and suggestions. To contact us, to receive a catalogue, or to be added to our mailing list please get in touch with us at:

SUTTON PUBLISHING
Phoenix Mill
Thrupp
Stroud
Glos
GL5 2BU

Tel: 01453-731114
e-mail: sales@sutton-publishing.co.uk